A History of the Congress of Roman Frontier Studies 1949-2024

ARCHAEOLOGICAL LIVES

A History of the Congress of Roman Frontier Studies 1949-2024

David J. Breeze, Tatiana Ivleva,
Rebecca H. Jones and Andreas Thiel

ARCHAEOPRESS PUBLISHING · OXFORD
2024

Archaeopress Publishing Ltd
Summertown Pavilion
18-24 Middle Way
Summertown
Oxford OX2 7LG
www.archaeopress.com

ISBN 978-1-80327-817-9
ISBN 978-1-80327-818-6 (e-Pdf)

© Archaeopress and David J. Breeze, Tatiana Ivleva, Rebecca H. Jones, Andreas Thiel and those who provided reminiscences 2024

First edition 2022
This edition 2024

Cover images: The participants at the First Congress in 1949 and the Twenty-fifth Congress in 2022

The authors and publishers are grateful to the Municipality of Nijmegen, the Netherlands for their support towards the publication of the first edition of this book. We are further grateful to the Cultural Heritage Preservation Agency of Ajara, Georgia, for their support enabling this second edition to be published.

All rights reserved. No part of this book may be reproduced, or transmitted, in any form or by any means, electronic, mechanical, photocopying or otherwise, without the prior written permission of the copyright owners.
This book is available direct from Archaeopress or from our website www.archaeopress.com

For Siegmar von Schnurbein

who led the Congress of Roman Frontier Studies for many years

Contents

List of figures iii
Preface 1
    Preface to the second edition 2
Introduction 3
The Sixth International Congress of Archaeology, Berlin 1939 6
The First Congress, Newcastle, England, UK 1949 13
The Second Congress, Carnuntum, Austria 1955 21
The Third Congress, Rheinfelden/Basel, Switzerland 1957 23
The Fourth Congress, Durham, England, UK 1959 26
The Fifth Congress, former Yugoslavia 1961 28
The Sixth Congress, Arnoldshain, Germany 1964 31
The Seventh Congress, Tel Aviv, Israel 1967 36
The Eighth Congress, Cardiff, Wales, UK 1969 39
The Ninth Congress, Mamaïa, Romania 1972 43
The Tenth Congress, Xanten and Nijmegen, Germany and the Netherlands 1974 47
The Eleventh Congress, Székesfehérvár, Hungary 1976 54
The Twelfth Congress, Stirling, Scotland, UK 1979 58
The Thirteenth Congress, Aalen, Germany 1983 66
The Fourteenth Congress, Carnuntum, Austria 1986 73
The Fifteenth Congress, Canterbury, England, UK 1989 80
The Sixteenth Congress, Rolduc Abbey, Kerkrade, the Netherlands 1995 85
The Seventeenth Congress, Zalău, Romania 1997 91
The Eighteenth Congress, Amman, Jordan 2000 97
The Nineteenth Congress, Pécs, Hungary 2003 106
The Twentieth Congress, León, Spain 2006 113
The Twenty-First Congress, Newcastle, England, UK 2009 119
The Twenty-second Congress, Ruse, Bulgaria 2012 126
The Twenty-third Congress, Ingolstadt, Germany 2015 134
The Twenty-fourth Congress, Viminacium, Serbia 2018 142
The Twenty-fifth Congress, Nijmegen, the Netherlands 2022 151

Reflections on the Congress 157
    The structure of the Congress meetings... 157
    International influences... 159
    The cycle of meetings 160
    The location of Congresses 160
    Planning a Congress 164
    Special features... 165
        The logos 165
        The 'singing' bus 166
        Entertainment: the folk dancing and re-enactors 167
        Mementos 170
        A retrospective 176
The Frontiers of the Roman Empire World Heritage property 177
Further reading 186
Appendix 188
The frontiers of the Roman Empire multi-language books... 188
Acknowledgements... 190

List of figures

Figure 1. Map of the provinces and frontiers of the Roman Empire in the mid 2nd century AD 4
Figure 2. The 1929 excavations at Birdoswald 5
Figure 3. Participants at the Sixth International Congress of Archaeology relax in a beer garden in Berlin: Andreas Alföldi turning to his right with behind him and to the right seated Eric Birley and Howard Comfort with the bow tie 6
Figure 4. Table of attendance at the Congresses 8
Figure 5. Map of the locations of the Congresses 9
Figure 6. Covers of some of the Congress proceedings 11
Figure 7. Eric Birley with his wife Peggy and John Gillam and Brenda Swinbank 12
Figure 8. The participants in the First Congress at Newcastle (1949) 14
Figure 9. Anne Robertson, first female speaker at the Limes Congress 16
Figure 10. Guda van Giffen-Duyvis and Albert Egges van Giffen in 1949 at the Congress 17
Figure 11. International delegates at the First Congress 18
Figure 12. The museum at Augst (*Augusta Raurica*) 24
Figure 13. Another view of the museum at Augst 25
Figure 14. Four Congress stalwarts on the 1959 Pilgrimage of Hadrian's Wall 27
Figure 15. Sirmium, visited in 1961 28
Figure 16. Group photo of participants during the visit to Ptuj 30
Figure 17. The Evangelical Academy in Arnoldshain 31
Figure 18. Telegram from Prof Emil Condurachi from Bucharest asking for an entrance visa 32
Figure 19. Albert van Giffen Maurice Euzennat(?) and Arend Hubrecht 32
Figure 20. Communication at Arnoldshain 33
Figure 21. Hans Schönberger's hand-written copy of the Arnoldshain lecture program 34
Figure 22. Mordechai Gichon's formal invitation letter to host the next Congress in Tel Aviv 37
Figure 23. The 'high table' at the Congress in Tel Aviv 38
Figure 24. Congress participants attending a lecture in Israel in 1967 38
Figure 25. The visit to the fort at Brecon Gaer during the Welsh Congress 40
Figure 26. Visiting the excavations at Usk in South Wales 41
Figure 27. The paddle steamer *Decebal* passed on the Danube 44
Figure 28. The late Roman fort at Cappidava 44
Figure 29. Congress participants on a ferry to visit Dinogetia 45
Figure 30. Jules Bogaers, one of the organisers of the 1974 Congress 47

Figure 31.	Visiting an excavation at Xanten	48
Figure 32.	Harald von Petrikovits examining a section at Haltern in 1974	48
Figure 33.	Participants returning to the hotel ship moored at Xanten	49
Figure 34.	The Congress welcomed to the G.M. Kam Museum in Nijmegen by Arend Hubrecht	50
Figure 35.	Names of people identified in Figure 34	51
Figure 36.	Epigraphists at work at Nijmegen	51
Figure 37.	The fort of Tokod being inspected in 1976	54
Figure 38.	The Valentinianic watch-tower at Steinbruch, Visegrád	55
Figure 39.	*Contra Aquincum*, now covered over, in Budapest	56
Figure 40.	The Heidentor, visited on the pre-Congress tour of 1976	56
Figure 41.	David Breeze inviting next Congress to Scotland	58
Figure 42.	The core team for the Stirling Congress	59
Figure 43.	Visit to the watch-tower above Fendoch	60
Figure 44.	The visit to the fortlet at Duntocher	61
Figure 45.	The bath-house at Bearsden	61
Figure 46.	Bearsden bath-house explained in German	62
Figure 47.	John Wilkes' excavation at the Severan legionary base at Carpow	63
Figure 48.	An attentive audience in Aalen, 1983	67
Figure 49.	Sheet music of the 'March of Ala Flavia II'	68
Figure 50.	The timber tower at Mahdholz	68
Figure 51.	Margot Klee explains the fortlet at Welzheim, Rötelsee	69
Figure 52.	The late Roman fort at Zurzach	70
Figure 53.	Mordechai Gichon and C. Sebastian Sommer in Aalen	71
Figure 54.	Hermann Vetters with Eric Birley	73
Figure 55.	Guiding by Herma Stiglitz	73
Figure 56.	The Roman tower at Tulln	74
Figure 57.	Visiting the site of Zeiselmauer	75
Figure 58.	Guiding by Hannsjörg Ubl	76
Figure 59.	A Grubenhaus at Bratislava-Dúbravka, Slovakia	76
Figure 60.	Vivien Swan leads the singing at Canterbury in 1989	80
Figure 61.	The Roman lighthouse in Dover	81
Figure 62.	The late Roman fort at Portchester Castle	82
Figure 63.	The Ermine Street Guard on parade	82
Figure 64.	Tom Parker gets instructions from the Ermine Street Guard	83
Figure 65.	Peter Guest guiding	84
Figure 66.	The participants of the Congress at Rolduc, 1995	85
Figure 67.	The pre-Congress excursion in 1995 included a visit to Kalkriese	86
Figure 68.	The post-Congress tour in 1995 explored sites and excavations in Belgium	87
Figure 69.	Tongeren in 1995	88
Figure 70.	The forum at Bavay	88
Figure 71.	Alexandru Matei explaining his excavation in 1997	91

Figure 72.	Group photo of congress participants from Zalău Congress	92
Figure 73.	Walking through the Carpathian Mountains in Romania	92
Figure 74.	Relaxing after a long walk	93
Figure 75.	The army provided lunch at Porolissum	94
Figure 76.	Inside the tent; standing Willem Willems	94
Figure 77.	Inspecting an excavation at Alba Iulia on the post-Congress excursion	95
Figure 78.	HRH Prince Hassan arrives to welcome the Congress to Jordan	97
Figure 79.	The Congress in Jordan	98
Figure 80.	Siegmar von Schnurbein addresses the Congress	98
Figure 81.	Colin Wells at Qasr el-Azraq	100
Figure 82.	Crossing the desert to visit Qasr Bshir	100
Figure 83.	Tom Parker greets the Congress	101
Figure 84.	Gabriele Rasbach, Andreas Thiel, Kirsten Thiel and Franz B. Maier at the British Ambassador's reception.	102
Figure 85.	Rebecca Jones, Fraser Hunter, Carol Davies and Jeff Davies at the British Ambassador's reception	102
Figure 86.	Mark Steel, Walter and Helen Cockle and Roberta Tomlin at the British Ambassador's reception	102
Figure 87.	David Kennedy with David Breeze and Zsolt Visy	103
Figure 88.	Delegates boarding the helicopter for a flight over Amman and Jerash	103
Figure 89.	Martina Meyr in the desert	105
Figure 90.	Zsolt Visy gets the Congress delegates ready for a group photograph	106
Figure 91.	Participants discuss applying for European funding for the Frontiers of the Roman Empire project	107
Figure 92.	Local school children perform a dance for the delegates	108
Figure 93.	Visiting the Roman fort at *Gerulata* on the pre-Congress excursion	109
Figure 94.	80th birthday celebrations for Klára Póczy with a presentation from Orsolya Lang	110
Figure 95.	Tony Wilmott and other Congress delegates waving the flags at León	113
Figure 96.	Eduard Nemeth, Ioana Bogdan Cătăniciu, Felix Marcu and Ovidiu Tentea in Spain	114
Figure 97.	The spectacular landscape of the Roman mines at Las Médulas	114
Figure 98.	Esperanza Martín and Ángel Morillo explaining Numancia	115
Figure 99.	Boris Rankov and Geoff Morley taking the ultimate photo looking up the Tower at A Coruña	116
Figure 100.	David Breeze at the wooden carving of Scotland's Stone of Destiny in the Council Chamber at A Coruña	117
Figure 101.	Matt Symonds on a bus between sites	118
Figure 102.	Congress participants at the closing assembly	120
Figure 103.	Nick Hodgson at Piercebridge	120
Figure 104.	Paul Bidwell explaining Piercebridge	120

Figure 105.	David Petts explains Binchester	121
Figure 106.	Visit to Whitley Castle	122
Figure 107.	Visiting the Roman cemetery of Petty Knowes near High Rochester	122
Figure 108.	Post-Congress tour at Chesters	122
Figure 109.	Bill Hanson explains the watch-tower of Muir O'Fauld	123
Figure 110.	Lyudmil Vagalinski	126
Figure 111.	Danish scholars at teh congress	127
Figure 112.	Congress participants relaxing by the Danube after a visit to the Roman fort *Dimum*	127
Figure 113.	Florian Matei-Popescu, George Cupcea, Călin Timoc enjoying lunch	128
Figure 114.	Nicolae Gudea at Medzhidy Tabiya	128
Figure 115.	Piotr Dyczek explains the fortress at *Novae*	129
Figure 116.	*Legio I Italica* at *Novae* (Svishtov)	129
Figure 117.	Carol van Driel-Murray at *Sexaginta Prista*	130
Figure 118.	Martin Lemke and Sebastian Sommer at Ruse	131
Figure 119.	Sebastian Sommer addresses the Congress	134
Figure 120.	The Congress participants gathered at the fort at Eining	135
Figure 121.	The 'Freiburger Truppe' from Freiburg University at Ingolstadt	135
Figure 122.	The miniature reconstruction at Ruffenhofen	136
Figure 123.	Boat trip on the Danube	137
Figure 124.	Markus Gschwind introduces the fort at Eining	137
Figure 125.	Some of the Limes ladies at the Kelten- & Römermuseum at Manching	138
Figure 126.	The limes at Zandt: watch-tower 15/15	138
Figure 127.	Walking in fog to visit the *limes* at Zandt	139
Figure 128.	The high table at the opening ceremony in Belgrade	142
Figure 129.	Delegates catching up in Belgrade at the start of the Congress	144
Figure 130.	The entrance to the replica Roman fort at Viminacium	144
Figure 131.	Boris Burandt gives a lecture	145
Figure 132.	The winner of the debate in Viminacium	146
Figure 133.	Visiting the Iron Gates in Serbia	147
Figure 134.	The Congress participants at the Roman fort of *Diana*	146
Figure 135.	Visiting the late Roman / Byzantine city of *Justiniana Prima*	148
Figure 136.	A reception in the courtyard of the replica Roman villa – the *Domus Scientiarum Viminacium*	149
Figure 137.	Fireworks at the end of the closing session	149
Figure 138.	The Congress participants gathered in the amphitheatre at the Archäologischen Park Xanten, Germany.	153
Figure 139.	The De Meern 1 ship on display at Castellum Hoge Woerd.	153
Figure 140.	The signing of the letter of intent towards the realisation of a National Roman Maritime Museum at Museumpark Archeon	154
Figure 141.	David Breeze receiving his lifetime achievement award.	155
Figure 142.	Leaflets and books from the 2003 Congress	161

Figure 143.	David Breeze receiving his Festschrift in Newcastle in 2009	162
Figure 144.	The celebration for the launch of Bill Hanson's Festschrift in Ingolstadt in 2015	162
Figure 145.	Bill Hanson receiving his Festschrift	163
Figure 146.	Carol van Driel-Murray receiving her Festschrift	163
Figure 147.	Collage of the logos from the Congresses	165
Figure 148.	Tom Parker leads the singing on the bus in 2015	167
Figure 149.	Two of the re-enactors greeting Congress participants at Binchester	168
Figure 150.	Re-enactors dressed as soldiers greet participants at Binchester	168
Figure 151.	Actors following the 'fight' between the Romans and Iron Age people in Viminacium	168
Figure 152.	Children doing traditional dances during the Congress in Bulgaria in 2012	169
Figure 153.	The stamped samian bowl from Pécs reading: MMDCCLVI SOPIANAE	170
Figure 154.	Bags for delegates for the 2018 *Viminacium* and 2015 Ingolstadt Congresses	171
Figure 155.	Some of the T-shirts spotted at the Congress	171
Figure 156.	Proportion of male/female delegates in the last 30 years	172
Figure 157.	Gender balance by province	172
Figure 158.	Gender balance by topic	174
Figure 159.	Baby Ariana accompanying her mother Renate Kurzmann to the Limes Congress in Jordan in 2000	175
Figure 160.	Frontiers of the Roman Empire Culture 2000 partners at their first meeting in Sopron, Hungary, in 2005	178
Figure 161.	Frontiers of the Roman Empire Culture 2000 partners meet with colleagues from the Netherlands	179
Figure 162.	Anna Adamczyk holding four of the books launched at the Congress in 2022	180
Figure 163.	Erik Dobat and Sandra Walkshofer filming in Bulgaria in 2007	180
Figure 164.	Final workshop of the Advanced Limes Applications project in Landshut, Bavaria in 2019	182
Figure 165.	Building the The '*Danuvia Alacris*' replica ship which rowed down the Danube in 2022	182
Figure 166.	The UNESCO World Heritage branding outside the Tullie House Museum and Art Gallery in Carlisle	182
Figure 167.	The UNESCO nomination team for the Danube Limes (western segment) visiting the wall of Regensburg legionary fortress	183
Figure 168.	Hadrian's Wall visit to the Great Wall of China in 2019 as part of the Wall-to-Wall project	184
Figure 169.	The organisers of the Nijmegen and Batumi congresses after the closing ceremony in Nijmegen in August 2022	191

A note on terminology. The Congress is referred to as the International Congress of Roman Frontier Studies or Limes Congress or Limeskongress. 'Limes' is the Roman term for a frontier, though, just to complicate matters, it originally meant a road. In this book, we will refer to the Limes Congress, but when referring to the frontier, *limes* will be used, as in the German *limes*. Even this leads to complications because the correct name for the World Heritage Property is the 'Obergermanisch-Raetischer Limes'. We crave the indulgence of our readers for our efforts in seeking uniformity of expression.

The Congress has also taken place over a period of time when several countries have changed their names. We have attempted to retain some consistency but, again, have made a judgement call and hope our readers can tolerate some of our decisions.

Preface

In 1949, in the aftermath of a devastating war, Eric Birley organised the First Congress of Roman Frontier Studies. His aim was not only to pursue the study of Roman frontiers but also to take a step towards restoring harmony in international relations within this field of research. Complete delivery of his aim was not possible as several German archaeologists were still Prisoners of War in Soviet Union. These include Kurt Stade, with whom Birley had planned the First Congress in Berlin in 1939 while attending the Sixth International Archaeology Congress. Stade had excavated with Birley at Birdoswald on Hadrian's Wall in 1929, together with Ian Richmond and Shimon Applebaum. The friendships formed there were to last through decades and Applebaum went on to organise the Seventh Congress in Tel Aviv in 1967 and attend its successor in Cardiff in 1969.

The pattern had been set early on: the exchange of information, networking and friendship. These three elements remain at the core of the approach of those organising and attending the Congress. They are reinforced by the pattern of the meetings, usually held every three years. The programme includes not only lectures but also visits to the local Roman military sites led by appropriate specialists. Over several Congresses, it is possible to inspect many of the iconic Roman military installations around the Roman Empire, and in particular observe them in their landscape settings. Alas, however, not all, as it has proved impossible to hold a Congress in North Africa and several of the countries of the Middle East.

Over the 73 years since the First Congress, membership has grown enormously with more lecture theatres and more coaches being required every meeting. In this year of publication, 2022, we hold the twenty-fifth Congress at Nijmegen in the Netherlands, a city well known to Roman frontier archaeologists and early medieval scholars alike. Here, we anticipate that around 400 archaeologists will gather to continue their voyages of exploration. For newer participants, we hope this book will help them understand the body they have joined; for older friends, this will be a reminder of friendships made and strengthened; for all, we trust that it will be a spur to continuing investigations and research into Rome's greatest monument, its frontiers; for this year, it will be a celebration of the twenty-fifth Congress of Roman Frontier Studies.

The exercise of creating this book has made us realise that there are greater stories to be told than in these pages, through the development of the study of Roman frontiers and the role of the Congress of Roman Frontier Studies in this process. This story is populated by many of the well-known archaeologists of the last 75 years and, indeed, earlier as the genesis of the Congress lies in the inter-War years. It is also a story of international cooperation and redemption. In preparing this book, we have used known archives, such as that at Vindolanda, as well as that maintained by the first author and now donated to the Römisch-Germanische Kommission in Frankfurt. We have also discovered other archives, such as that of Albert Egges van Giffen in the library of Groningen University and Eric Birley's file at the Deutsches Archäologisches Institut, and no doubt others exist. These archives, covering the whole history of the Congress, stand ready for further study.

David J. Breeze, Edinburgh
Tatiana Ivleva, Leiden
Rebecca H. Jones, Peebles
Andreas Thiel, Esslingen

Preface to the second edition

The first edition of this volume was produced in 2022 to mark the 25th Congress of Roman Frontiers Studies at Nijmegen in the Netherlands. Thanks to sponsorship from the Municipality of Nijmegen, every participant at the Congress was given a copy. Feedback on the volume and subsequent research has led to new information coming to light which has been incorporated in this second edition. This has been most notable in the identification of people on a photograph at that first Congress in 1949 (Cover and Figure 8). The authors welcome additional information on past conferences, in particular on participants, especially those who can be identified on photographs such as those on Figures 16 and 34. Tatiana Ivleva undertook the bulk of the editing work of this second edition with Rebecca Jones providing the report on the Nijmegen Congress.

Introduction

The remains of Roman frontiers lie in Europe, the Middle East and North Africa, physical manifestations of Rome's imperial policy (Figure 1). Known and recorded in various ways for centuries, it was the development of archaeological activities in the 19th century that brought them to greater attention. The history of research into the various frontiers around the Empire is full of the names of famous scholars. They include John Collingwood Bruce on Hadrian's Wall, Flóris Rómer in Hungary, Rudolf Brünnow and Alfred von Domaszewski in Jordan, Antoine Poidebard in Syria, Aurel Stein in Iraq and Jordan and of course, Theodor Mommsen in Germany and beyond, whose magnum opus on Römische Geschichte (*History of Rome*) was one reason for his award of the second Nobel Prize for Literature in 1902. The *Corpus Inscriptionum Latinarum* (*CIL*) that he established remains the authoritative source for Roman epigraphy.

It was Mommsen's agitation for *Limes* research that led to the foundation of the Reichs-Limeskommission (RLK) in 1892. Two years earlier, in 1890, the Glasgow Archaeological Society had undertaken seminal excavations on the Antonine Wall; also in the 1890s, the Oxford scholar Francis Haverfield started his research on Hadrian's Wall. This and subsequent decades were formative in establishing archaeological understanding of Roman frontiers.

Research into the archaeological phenomena of the border provinces of the Roman Empire continued to gain prominence into the 20th century. The German scholar Ernst Fabricius, (head of the RLK from 1902) was in regular contact with Eric Birley from Britain, whose lifelong interest in Hadrian's Wall began whilst a student at Oxford in the 1920s and further developed during his tenure at Durham University. Fabricius sent his assistant, Kurt Stade, to the excavations at Birdoswald in 1929 (Figure 2). These excavations became famous for the artefacts and inscriptions uncovered, which influenced research on Hadrian's Wall for some 50 years.

Figure 1. Map of the provinces and frontiers of the Roman Empire in the mid 2nd century AD (produced for the Frontiers of the Roman Empire EU Culture 2000 project)

Figure 2. The 1929 excavations at Birdoswald, from left to right, John Charlton, Eric Birley, Mr Hunter a student, F.G. Simpson, Mr Addison a student, Kurt Stade, Shimon Applebaum, R.G. Collingwood. Ian Richmond took the photograph

The Sixth International Congress of Archaeology, Berlin 1939

In August 1939, around eight hundred participants from 34 nations joined the Sixth International Congress of Archaeology in Berlin. Among the scientists who met at the invitation of the Deutsches Archäologisches Institut were Andreas Alföldy, Eric Birley, Howard Comfort, Hans Dragendorff and many other familiar names in Roman archaeology (Figure 3).

One of the six sessions held at that Congress was on 'Roman Antiquity II – The north and west'. In his opening speech, Rudolph Egger of Vienna set out the motives

Figure 3. Participants at the Sixth International Congress of Archaeology relax in a beer garden in Berlin: Andreas Alföldi turning to his right with behind him and to the right seated Eric Birley and Howard Comfort with the bow tie

behind this special section: 'The reason is not due to external circumstances, e. g. the abundance of material, ... but to the close relations that connect the west of Europe and the Danube countries ... Emphasis should also be placed on ... the distinct independent existence of these provinces...', a confident statement at a time when 'archaeology' was seen as the archaeology of ancient Egypt and Greece.

Nineteen speakers introduced archaeological, historical and numismatic research from Algeria, Austria, Germany, Yugoslavia, Poland, Romania, Switzerland, Serbia, Hungary and the United Kingdom. Several of these were genuine frontier papers. They included Christoph Albrecht on Oberaden, Andreas Alföldi on the Sarmatians, Viktor Hoffiller on Sirmium, Louis Leschi on Lambaesis, Stefan Paulivics on Aquincum and Nicola Vulić on the Danube *limes*. Papers on Roman frontiers were given in other sessions, on Adamklissi, the Citadel in Jerusalem and the frontier system of Arabia and Palestine.

Surviving letters in the Deutsches Archäologisches Institut in Berlin demonstrate that since at least 1937 Eric Birley, Ian Richmond and Kurt Stade had been discussing the possibility of holding the First Congress of Roman Frontier Studies in Britain to follow the Pilgrimage of Hadrian's Wall in 1940 (RGK-A-0373 55a-b). Birley and Stade continued the discussions at the International Congress of Archaeology. But, given the timing of the Congress, August 1939, Eric Birley was there but briefly, having to leave it in a hurry, summoned back to Britain via a coded telegram purportedly sent by his wife but actually from Military Intelligence, who had recruited him three or four months earlier because of his excellent German and study of the Roman army. In his haste, he left his pyjamas behind. After the War they were returned to him by Frau Nesselhauf, washed and ironed.

Turning plans into reality

Needless to say, the Second World War prevented the holding of both the Congress and the Pilgrimage in 1940. But after the War had ended, the time was ripe for a specific Congress on the archaeological issues of the Roman border provinces. Birley resurrected the proposal with the intention of bringing together colleagues from across Europe, restoring international relations and rebuilding harmony between nations. Unfortunately, Kurt Stade could not attend because he was still a Prisoner of War in the Soviet Union.

The first International Congress of Roman Frontier Studies was held in Newcastle upon Tyne in July 1949 and timed to follow the Centenary Pilgrimage of Hadrian's Wall. It was a small gathering of about 40 archaeologists and historians (together with several spouses), but it included significant figures such as Andreas Alföldi and Mortimer Wheeler. Today, up to 400 people from 25 countries and all five continents come together in a province of the Roman Empire to discuss recent research into Roman frontier archaeology, artefacts, frontier social worlds, Roman military studies and visit the frontier remains and museums in the area in which the Congress is being held (Figure 4).

The relationship between that Centenary Pilgrimage and the First Congress set the pattern for many future meetings in that the Pilgrimage served as a pre- or post-Congress tour in the ninth year of each decade thereby drawing the Congress back to Britain. This ran for five decades, but after 1989 it was decided to break the link and hold the Congress every three years; in 2009 the two patterns coincided again and the Congress returned to Newcastle, the location of that First Congress sixty years earlier. At many Congresses there has been a pre- and a post-Congress tour of sites

Jahr, Ort	Participants	Lectures	Lectures published
1949, Newcastle (GB)	40	11	11
1955, Carnuntum (AT)	34	22	22
1957, Rheinfelden (CH)		21	20
1959, Durham (GB)	89	20	
1961, Celje (SL)	69	25	19
1964, Arnoldshain (DE)	100	27	27
1967, Tel Aviv (IL)	84	41	37
1969, Cardiff (GB)	103	32	32
1972, Mamaia (RO)	177	69	55
1974, Xanten/Nijmegen (DE/NL)	180	68	68
1976, Székesfehérvár (HU)	156	87	57
1979, Stirling (GB)	164	81	77
1983, Aalen (DE)	284	120	115
1986, Carnuntum (AT)	225	104	87
1989, Canterbury (GB)	190	102	100
1995, Rolduc (NL)	200	99	99
1997, Zalău (RO)	204	106	106
2000, Amman (JO)	250	150	100
2003, Pécs (HU)	240	150	99
2006, León (ES)	284	197	138
2009, Newcastle (GB)	350	180	105
2012, Ruse (BG)	300	204	127
2015, Ingolstadt (DE)	370	210	149
2018, Viminacium (RS)	360	260	140
2022, Nijmegen (NL)	441	246	186

Figure 4. Table of attendance at the Congresses. The figures in pink are unknown and those in yellow are unconfirmed

The Sixth International Congress of Archaeology, Berlin 1939

Figure 5. Map of the locations of the Congresses.
Newcastle, Durham, Cardiff, Stirling and Canterbury (UK); Carnuntum (Austria); Rheinfelden/Basel (Switzerland); Arnoldshain, Aalen and Ingolstadt (Germany); Tel Aviv (Israel); Mamaïa and Zalău (Romania); Székesfehérvár and Pécs (Hungary); Rolduc Abbey, Kerkrade (Netherlands) Amman (Jordan); León (Spain); Ruse (Bulgaria); and Viminacium (Serbia) with the Congresses often travelling around, such as the Xanten and Nijmegen Congress (Germany and Netherlands) and one in the former Yugoslavia (listed as Celje on the map).

and museums, normally lasting between one and three days, thereby extending the whole Congress experience up to a fortnight.

A distinct feature of the Congress since the first meeting has been the integration of lectures and site tours, the latter helping to ensure the convivial atmosphere which is the hallmark of the Congress. Over the last 73 years the Congress has travelled to 15 countries in Europe from the Atlantic to the Black Sea and two in the Middle East. In Roman terms, an equivalent number of provinces have been visited (Figure 5).

It is a matter of great regret that a full Congress has not been held in North Africa. In 1954, the exciting discoveries in North Africa beckoned but the death of the organiser Louis Leschi led to its cancellation. The unsettled international situation led a proposed Congress in Morocco in 2018 to be abandoned. The interests of the participants of the Congress has always extended to the lands beyond the frontier and the artefacts found there that had passed through Roman frontiers.

The Congress of Roman Frontier Studies is unusual in that it has no constitution, although a Code of Conduct has recently been issued. At each meeting, the location of the next Congress is decided at a plenary session and the baton passes from the organisers of that Congress to those who will prepare the next (though whenever possible Congresses are planned two ahead). Each Congress is organised by a local Committee but advised by an 'international committee' consisting of those archaeologists who have organised previous meetings. Continuity is also provided by the two chairs of the Congress, recently David Breeze and Siegmar von Schnurbein and now Rebecca Jones and Andreas Thiel. The local Committee take on the bulk of the organisation, and are responsible for seeing through the subsequent publication of their Acta, the proceedings of the Congress (Figure 6). It is incredible that two scholars who attended the First Congress in Newcastle in 1949 are still alive: Brenda Heywood (Figure 7) and Norman McCord. The reminiscences of those who attended the Congresses are an important part of our history and so we have invited some colleagues to offer their memories of a key meeting, often the First Congress they attended, although more were submitted and most included below.

This book considers each Congress in turn against the political background of the time. Essential information is provided at the beginning of each account with a bibliography of the Congress at the end. The first item is the proceedings of the Congress, followed by the guide for the Congress, when one was produced, and finally additional publications relating to the Congress. These include reviews, several of which contain critical comments not just on the publications but on the nature of the Congress itself.

The gathering of information on each Congress has not always been easy. In the early days, information on the organisation and organisers of the Congress was frequently not provided, and one report does not even have an editor cited. However,

The Sixth International Congress of Archaeology, Berlin 1939

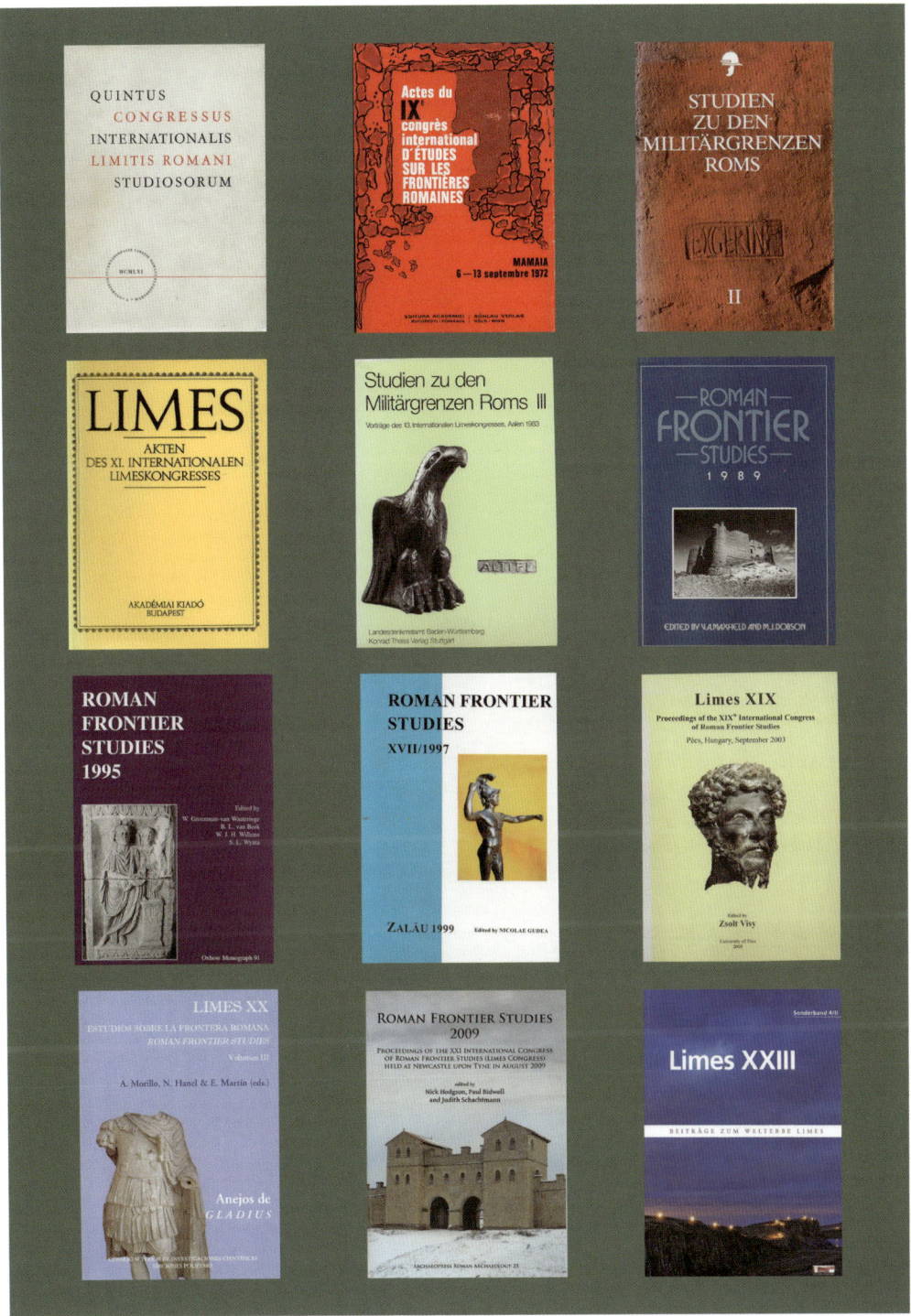

Figure 6. Covers of some of the Congress proceedings

Figure 7. Eric Birley with his wife Peggy and John Gillam (far left) and Brenda Swinbank (later Heywood, far right)

this gradually changed with the editor of the proceedings often providing not only an overview of the event (from 1989 onwards) but also a review of research on the frontiers in his/her country and comment on the impact of the visit of the Congress (starting in 2003). These are valuable accounts in their own right, but also provide useful information on the development of the conferences and therefore an aspect of the history of archaeology in the 20th century and into the 21st.

The First Congress, Newcastle, England, UK 1949

The Congress ran from Monday 11 to Thursday 14 July. The meeting was based in Newcastle – at that time, Newcastle University was not yet in existence and was Kings College of Durham University. The Congress was preceded by the Centenary Pilgrimage of Hadrian's Wall, which ran from Monday 5 to Saturday 10 July. It was in the Roman province of Britannia.

The Congress was timed to follow immediately after the Centenary Pilgrimage of Hadrian's Wall. This allowed the participants in the Congress to attend the Pilgrimage and be introduced to the Wall and the work undertaken along it since the previous Pilgrimage in 1930. All but one of the speakers at the Congress attended the Pilgrimage. The absentee was Albert Egges van Giffen whose leg was in plastercast following the recent car accident in Germany, but his wife Guda van Giffen-Duyvis attended the Pilgrimage.

The Congress was sponsored by the Society of Antiquaries of Newcastle, the Cumberland and Westmorland Antiquarian and Archaeological Society, the Society of Antiquaries of London, the Society of Antiquaries of Scotland, the Cambrian Archaeological Association and the Society for the Promotion of Roman Studies.

About 40 participants travelled to Newcastle from as far afield as Algeria and Denmark (Figure 8). There were eleven speakers, ten of whom were from Europe, with the eleventh, Frenchman Jean Baradez from Algiers in French Algeria (which was still part of France until its independence in 1962). Speakers from the UK were Eric Birley (University of Durham), V. E. Nash-Williams (National Museum of Wales and University College, Cardiff), Mortimer Wheeler (Institute of Archaeology, London), and Anne S. Robertson (University of Glasgow), the latter was the only female speaker (Figure 9). There were two speakers from Germany: Ulrich Kahrstedt (University of Göttingen) and Franz Oelmann (Bonn State Museum); Hans Norling-Christensen attended from the University of Copenhagen in Denmark; Rudolf Laur-Belart came from Switzerland (University of Basel); Albert Egges van Giffen from the Netherlands (University of Groningen), and Antonio Frova from Italy, where he worked for the Superintendent of Antiquities for Lombardy in Milan, but reported on the Italian Archaeological Expedition to Bulgaria in the early 1940s (in 1961, an inscription recording *Po]ntius Pilatus* was found during his excavations in Israel). The Hungarian scholar Andreas Alföldi had recently emigrated from Budapest to the University of Bern in Switzerland because of the post-war influence of the Soviet Union over the Hungarian state. His published paper on 'The moral barrier on Rhine and Danube' is the most quoted today from that first publication of the Limes Congress proceedings (Alföldi 1952).

Figure 8. The participants in the First Congress at Newcastle (1949). The photo was probably taken in the garden of Tullie House Museum, Carlisle, preceding the Congress on the Pilgrimage's last day. Seated on the ground from the left: Howard Comfort (?), Willem Glasbergen, Anne S. Robertson, Barbara Birley, Eric Birley, Ian Richmond, Andreas Alföldi, unknown, unknown. Standing in the middle row: Lieutenant-Colonel George R. B. Spain, Franz Oelmann, Georg 'Gyuri' Kunwald (?), Christopher Hawkes, unknown, unknown, Ulrich Kahrstedt, Rev. Thomas Romans, Robert Hogg, Katherine 'Kate' Hodgson; Margerie V. Taylor, unknown, unknown, Jocelyn Toynbee, Grace Simpson, Philip Corder, unknown. Standing in the back row: unknown, John Morris, unknown, unknown, Hans Norling-Christensen, Colonel Jean Baradez, Antonio Frova, Guda van Giffen-Duyvis, Mortimer Wheeler, Victor Erle Nash-Williams, unknown, Derek Siddle. Many Congress participants are wearing the round 1949 Pilgrimage badge. Several people recorded elsewhere as having attended the Congress are not on this photograph: Shimon Applebaum; Norman McCord; F.G. Simpson; Brenda Swinbank (later Heywood); and Albert van Giffen. Martha Stewart has drawn our attention to a version of the photograph in which Eric Birley has pasted an image of F.G. Simpson over George Spain at the far left of the above photograph!

The papers embraced a good geographic spread across the Empire from the Antonine Wall to the Euphrates and included reports on recent work on the frontiers, early and late frontiers, and the effect of frontiers. One single paper by Hans Norling-Christensen addressed objects retrieved from beyond the frontiers.

Despite the geographic spread of the subjects, scholars either presented on research that was local to them or as a result of colonial occupations or international schools of research. Frova's investigations in Bulgaria (1901-3) were due to the work of the Italian Archaeological Expedition to Bulgaria and the Italian Institute in Sofia. Wheeler's reporting on Mesopotamia is in the manner of a colonial historian, and he concluded his paper with optimism for the future of research in the area due to the recent formal establishment of a British School of Archaeology in Iraq, noting a plea for an 'enterprising young scholar for equivalent work in northern Mesopotamia' (Wheeler 1952, 128). Incidentally, the reason for his optimism in Iraq was due to the appointment of Max Mallowan, who ran the school from 1947 to 1961 and was married to the author Agatha Christie, who set several of her novels in the Middle East.

Figure 9. Anne Robertson, first female speaker at the Limes Congress
(© The Herald (Glasgow))

Colonel Jean Baradez was part of the Directorate of Antiquities of French colonial Algeria where he carried out aerial surveys and excavations. He brought with him to the Congress the first copies of his seminal work on the *Fossatum Africae*. In his introduction to the Congress proceedings, Eric Birley emphasised the importance of the work of Baradez in North Africa, stating that his was the most exciting communication at the Congress. Eleven papers were published in 1952, all in English, although some were originally delivered in German and Italian. The volume included maps, but no photographs. Christopher Hawkes wrote a brief report in *The Archaeological News Letter* noting that 'the line of the Roman frontier-works [were] previously almost unknown, in Northern Africa', and noting the links between the Antonine Wall and Hadrian's Wall in Britain.

Anne S. Robertson was the only female speaker and Brenda Heywood (nee Swinbank) also attended the Congress, yet the photo of the Congress participants (Figure 8) shows that eight more women were present. We have been able to identify all but two of them, prominent archaeologists in their own right. Katherine ('Kate') Sophia Hodgson was the first female President of the Cumberland and Westmorland Antiquarian and Archaeological Society (CWAAS) (from 1948 to 1951). She is well known in Cumbrian archaeological circles for her publications of her fieldwork in the *Transactions of the CWAAS* on and around Hadrian's Wall, co-authoring papers with (amongst others) Ian Richmond, F.G. Simpson and Eric Birley. Guda van Giffen-Duyvis, wife of Dutch archaeologist Albert van Giffen (Figure 10), was a Dutch anthropologist, who published amongst others about Aztecs and pre-Columbian art of Mexico and Peru. Grace Simpson, a daughter of F.G. Simpson, at the time of the Congress was 29 years of age, and trained as an archaeologist right after the Second World War. One of her later publications

Figure 10. Guda van Giffen-Duyvis and Albert Egges van Giffen in 1949 at the Congress

Figure 11. International delegates at the First Congress. The photo was taken preceding the Congress during the Pilgrimage's visit to the Chesters Bridge Abutment. From the left: Franz Oelmann, Ulrich Kahrstedt, Colonel Jean Baradez, Antonio Frova, Guda van Giffen-Duyvis, Andreas Alföldi, Willem Glasbergen, Hans Norling-Christensen and possibly Georg Kunwald.

was *Watermills and Military Works on Hadrian's Wall*, which is a report and review of her father's earlier excavations. In 1950 she joined the Archaeology Department at Durham University, working as assistant to Eric Birley, and in the same year she became the Honorary Curator of the Clayton Collection of antiquities of Chesters Roman fort. She is the co-author of an essential reference volume on Roman Samian ware, *Central Gaulish Potters* (1958). Jocelyn Toynbee was the leading scholar in classical archaeology and Romano-British art, who at the time of the Congress was a lecturer and director of studies in classics at Newnham College, Cambridge. She is particularly known for her works *Art in Roman Britain* (1962), *The Art of the Romans* (1965) and *Death and Burial in the Roman World* (1971). Margerie V. Taylor was at the time of the Congress editor of the *Journal of Roman Studies* and secretary of the Society for the Promotion of Roman Studies for nearly 25 years. Starting as an assistant to Francis Haverfield, upon his death becoming the journal editor, she further promoted the Romano-British studies by compiling the annual account of excavations conducted on Romano-British sites. Her services to the profession were recognised when she was elected as a first female vice-president of the Society of Antiquaries of London. The sixth person is Barbara Birley, sister to Eric Birley.

The relationship between the Pilgrimage and this First Congress set a pattern for meetings to come for the former served as a pre-Congress tour. During the Congress other visits were made (Figure 11), to the Roman town of Corbridge beside Hadrian's Wall and to the outpost fort of High Rochester.

It was suggested that the Congress might meet every five years, with a desire to go to Algeria in 1954, however, the death of Louis Leschi, the Director of Antiquities in Algeria, in early January 1954 led to its cancellation. Instead, Jean Baradez led a small group of archaeologists, including John Gillam and V.E. Nash-Williams from the UK, on a tour of Gemellae and the neighbouring stretches of the *Fossatum Africae* in April of that year, when the Congress was originally due to take place (Birley 1974). Nash-Williams turned up for a desert excursion complete with Homburg hat and umbrella. That day, for the first time in years, it poured with rain. Nash-Williams was a devout Anglican and everyone thought he must have a hotline above.

Publications

Birley, E. (ed.) 1952. *The Congress of Roman Frontier Studies 1949*. Durham: University of Durham.

Baradez, J. 1949 *Vue-aérienne de l'organisation romaine dans le Sud-Algérien: Fossatum Africae*. Paris: Arts et métiers graphiques.

Alföldi, A. 1952. 'The moral barrier on the Rhine and Danube', in E. Birley (ed.) *The Congress of Roman Frontier Studies 1949*: 1-16. Durham: University of Durham.

Wheeler, R.E.M. 1952. 'The Roman Frontier in Mesopotamia', in E. Birley (ed.) *The Congress of Roman Frontier Studies 1949*: 112-29. Durham: University of Durham.

Hawkes, C.F.C. 1949. 'The Centenary Pilgrimage of Hadrian's Wall and the First Congress of Roman Frontier Studies, Newcastle upon Tyne, July 1949', *The Archaeological News Letter* 2, 3: 72-3.

Anon. 1950. 'The Centenary Pilgrimage', *Transactions of the Cumberland and Westmorland Antiquarian and Archaeological Society*, 49: 196-202.

Lacey, W.K. 1953. 'Review of *The Congress of Roman Frontier Studies 1949*', in *Journal of Roman Studies* 43: 213-4.

Reminiscences

Norman McCord (UK)

I was not long out of school, still living at home in a North Shields house much damaged by bombing and with affectionate memories of close neighbours and friends as blitz victims. I was – with many others – astonished to see Germans and Italians welcomed at that First Congress in the way they were. I feel pretty sure that the First Congress was a useful lesson to me in more than one respect!

Maarten de Weerd as told to him by Willem Glasbergen (Netherlands)

During the Congress, Albert van Giffen was walking around with his leg in plaster cast. It did not bother him that much, well, at least this is what he said to Eric Birley, who was compassionately asking him if he needed any help. Van Giffen steadfastly replied: 'no', adding 'this is anyways 'walking plaster''. Van Giffen travelled to the Congress with his wife Guda and his protege Willem Glasbergen, who was at the time 26 years of age. Willem was so sick on the plane to Newcastle that he refused to travel by plane again till well into his 50s.

The Second Congress, Carnuntum, Austria 1955

The Congress ran from Monday 25 to Friday 29 July 1955 at Bad Deutsch-Altenburg and Petronell, the Roman Carnuntum, in Austria, in the Roman province of Pannonia Superior.

After the cancellation of the 1954 Algerian Congress, Erich Swoboda of the University of Graz in Austria stepped into the breach and invited colleagues to attend a meeting in Carnuntum the following year. Although not intended as a Congress, it was subsequently accepted as the second. It began exactly on the day when the Austrian State Treaty was ratified, the troops of the four victorious powers of the Second World War were withdrawn and Austria became sovereign again. The Congress was supported by the Federal Ministry of Education.

Several of the scholars who had attended the First Congress in Newcastle returned for this one: Baradez, Birley, Laur-Belart and Nash-Williams. There were 34 participants in total from ten countries, and the proceedings, published the following year, incorporated 22 papers on a wide range of topics (including ancient history, archaeology, epigraphy, pottery and coins) in four languages (English, French, German and Italian). As the review of the Congress report in the *Journal of Roman Studies* states: 'The lectures are concerned with the frontier problems of the Roman Empire, the subject liberally interpreted to include the hinterland as well as the actual line of contact with the enemy. ... Some of the twenty-two summaries are very short and provide no more than an indication of the themes dealt with.'

The move of the Congress from the UK to Carnuntum on the Danube opened attendance to new participants working in the Danube provinces and as a result Swoboda is credited with increasing the number of scholars interested in joining *Limesforschung* (Birley 1974, 3). As well as papers from the UK, Germany, Italy, Switzerland, France, including French Algeria, and the host country, Austria, there were papers from beyond the Iron Curtain and from different Republics in the Socialist Federal Republic of Yugoslavia. Antonín Salač from Prague spoke about an inscription from Bratislava, János Szilágyi (Budapest) about Aquincum, and the Yugoslavian papers featured two speakers from Zagreb (Andre Mohorovičić and Grga Novak) on Dalmatia, and Miodrag Grbić (Belgrade) on artefacts from Serbia. Many of these scholars had worked and studied in a variety of different countries prior to the Second World War and were well established figures in archaeology and ancient history. Hans-Georg Pflaum, now based in Paris and presenting a paper on Algerian archaeology, was a German of Jewish ancestry who had left Germany for Paris in 1933. Birley's paper on Hadrianic Frontier Policy is regarded as a classic by modern scholars of Hadrian.

Publication

Swoboda, E. (ed.) 1956. *Carnuntina. Ergebnisse der Forschung über die Grenzprovinzen des römischen Reiches*. Vorträge beim internationalen Kongress der Altertumsforscher Carnuntum 1955. Römische Forschungen in Niederösterreich 3. Graz/Köln: H. Bohlaus.

Raleigh Radford, C.A. 1957. 'Review of *Carnuntina ...*', in *Journal of Roman Studies* 47: 209.

The Third Congress, Rheinfelden/Basel, Switzerland 1957

The Congress ran from Monday 26 to Saturday 31 August 1957. It started in Rheinfelden but moved to Basel in Switzerland for the main sessions. It was held in the Roman province of Germania Superior.

The Congress was organised by Rudolf Laur-Belart of the University of Basel. It started in Rheinfelden but for the main sessions moved to Basel where the city and university were patrons. In his introduction to the Congress proceedings, Laur-Belart commented on the pivotal location of Basel as a frontier town at the junction where Switzerland, France and Germany met.

Several speakers at this Congress had also attended the First Congress, including Andreas Alföldy, now at Princeton, and Jean Baradez. But they were joined by new colleagues including Gerhard Bersu, recently retired from the Römisch-Germanische Kommission following his prolonged exile in Britain and Ireland, due to his Jewish ancestry. Bersu is regarded as one of the great German archaeologists of the 20th century. Another notable scholar attending for the first time was Harald von Petrikovits, who had been a prisoner of the Soviet Union during and after the War resulting in him missing the previous two Congresses. Von Petrikovits was subsequently credited with rebuilding the Museum at Bonn. Hans Schönberger, at that point Director of the Saalburg Museum before becoming Director of the Römisch-Germanische Kommission, also attended.

The lectures included overviews of several frontiers, army units, forts, inscriptions, coins, small finds, and excavations; there was a distinct emphasis on the late Roman period. Maria Radnoti-Alföldi presented on the Emperor Gallienus, notable not only as one of only two women giving a lecture at the Congress, but also because she had only recently fled Hungary after its uprising (Autumn 1956) for Munich. The other woman is Elisabeth Ettlinger. Together with Howard Comfort (who was present at the Sixth International Congress of Archaeology held in 1939 in Berlin), she co-founded and became first Secretary of the *Rei Cretariae Romanae Fautores* (RCRF: study of Roman pottery) which met for the first time a few days after the Congress (2 to 4 September) in Vindonissa Museum. Four other Limes scholars from the Congress went on to give papers at the RCRF and published in the Acta: Harald von Petrikovits and Hans Schönberger, as well as Hans Klumbach from Mainz and Frantisek Křížek from Brno in Czechoslovakia. Twenty papers in four languages (German, English, French and Italian) were published in the Congress Acta. With over thirty pages by far the most

Figure 12. The museum at Augst (*Augusta Raurica*) – newly created in the 1950s

comprehensive contribution, '*Remarques sur l'onomastique de Cirta*', was penned by the ancient historian Hans-Georg Pflaum, since 1956 directeur de recherche au Centre national de la recherche scientifique (CNRS).

In terms of site visits during the Congress, opportunities were provided for delegates to visit Augst (*Augusta Raurica*) with its new museum (Figures 12 and 13), the late fort at Zurzach, the legionary fortress at Windisch (*Vindonissa*) and the Celtic and Roman settlement of Avenches (*Aventicum*).

Publication

Laur-Belart, R. (ed.) 1959. *Limes-Studien. Vorträge des 3. Internationalen Limes-Kongresses in Rheinfelden/Basel 1957.* Basel: Schriften des Instituts für Ur- und Frühgeschichte der Schweiz 14.

Hartley, B.R. 1960. 'Review of *Limes-Studien ...*', in *Antiquity* 34, no. 13: 79-80.

Figure 13. Another view of the museum at Augst

The Fourth Congress, Durham, England, UK 1959

The fourth Congress was held in Durham from Sunday 10 to Friday 15 September 1959, in the Roman province of Britannia. It was preceded by the Pilgrimage of Hadrian's Wall which ran from Saturday 6 to Thursday 10 September. The post-Congress tour was to Scotland.

By now, the Congress had become an established date in the diaries of frontier archaeologists. As a result, the attendance had swelled to an impressive 89 delegates, helped by a large contingent from the UK. People came from Algeria, Austria, Belgium, Bulgaria, France, Germany, Israel, Italy, the Netherlands, Switzerland as well as the UK. They included Shimon Applebaum, who had excavated at Birdoswald on Hadrian's Wall in 1929 and also attended the First Congress in Newcastle. Originally from Britain, he was now an Israeli and later became principal organiser of the Seventh Congress in Tel Aviv. Kurt Stade, who had also been a member of the 1929 Birdoswald team and had been instrumental in Eric Birley's establishment of the Congress, now returned to Britain after an absence of 30 years. Other notable participants included, from Britain: Eric and Tony Birley, Charles Daniels, Brian Dobson, Lady (Aileen) Fox, John Gillam, Brian Hartley, Michael Jarrett, George Jobey, John Kent, Norman McCord, Iain MacIvor, John Mann (organiser), John Morris, Charles Phillips, Ian Richmond, Leo Rivet, Anne S. Robertson, Peter Salway, Kenneth Steer, C.E. Stevens, John Wilkes and Richard Wright; from Germany: Dietwulf Baatz, Hans-Jörg Kellner, Hans Klumbach, Robert Nierhaus, Harald von Petrikovits, Wilhelm Schleiermacher, Hans Schönberger and Günter Ulbert; from France: Jean Baradez (French Algeria), Juliette Moreau, Hans-Georg Pflaum and André Piganiol; from the Netherlands: Jules Bogaers and Clasina Isings; from Belgium: Joseph Mertens; from Switzerland: Elisabeth Ettlinger and Rudolph Laur-Belart; from Austria: Erich Swoboda; from Hungary: Aladár Radnóti; from Bulgaria: Teofil Ivanov; from Italy: Albino Garzetti and Lellia Ruggini; and from Israel: Mordechai Gichon. Ernst Badian, also attended – he was originally from Austria, studied in the UK and New Zealand but later moved to the United States.

Many of the foreign delegates had spent the previous week attending the Pilgrimage of Hadrian's Wall (Sunday 6 to Thursday 10 September, Figure 14). The Pilgrimage started in Carlisle and ended in Newcastle where a special exhibition was mounted by David Smith, Keeper, in the Museum of Antiquities.

The Congress started the next morning with lectures which lasted over four days from Friday 11 to Monday 14 September. The 20 papers embraced the whole of the frontiers of the Empire from the Antonine Wall in Scotland, along the northern frontier in Europe and beyond to the eastern frontier in Mesopotamia and south to North Africa and included a paper on 'Native settlements of the Roman period

Figure 14. Four Congress stalwarts on the 1959 Pilgrimage of Hadrian's Wall: John Gillam, C.E. Stevens, Tony Birley and Jean Baradez with Thomas Hepple, Ministry foreman, second from the right

in Northumberland'. The lectures were organised into specific themes: artificial frontiers and their component structures; economic development of the frontier districts; developments of the fourth century; and Rome beyond the frontiers. The British scholar David Oates gave a special lecture on Hatra (Iraq) as well as a paper on the frontier in Mesopotamia. Various issues combined to prevent the publication of the proceedings though a ten-page transcript of the lectures survives.

After the Congress, David Smith led an expedition to Scotland during which the excavations of Ian Richmond and J.K. St Joseph at the legionary fortress at Inchtuthil were visited.

The Fifth Congress, former Yugoslavia 1961

The Congress was held in several locations in the then Yugoslavia from Sunday 17 to Saturday 23 September in the Roman provinces of Pannonia Superior and Dalmatia. The pre-Congress excursion, from Monday 11 to Saturday 16 September, was to Istria and Dalmatia, and the post-Congress tour, from Saturday 23 to Thursday 28 September, to Upper Moesia.

The Congress was held under the leadership of the Croatian archaeologist Grga Novak, who was President of the Yugoslav Academy of Sciences and Arts (Zagreb). The site visits embraced all constituent parts of former Yugoslavia. The Congress was therefore always on the move with never more than two nights spent in the same location. Delegates stayed in hotels, sometimes the Cooperative Hotel, and on-board steamers. The days could be long, arrival at the accommodation on one day being after 23.00, while the remains of the Bridge of Apollodorus over the Danube were inspected by moonlight.

The pre-Congress tour started in Ljubljana (*Emona*, Slovenia) where the archaeological museum was explored. At Poreč (*Parentium*, Croatia) the basilica was inspected and at Pula (*Pola*, Croatia) the amphitheatre and other Roman remains. Transport to Split was by steamer; after inspecting Diocletian's Palace, the group moved on to the town of Solin (*Salonae*, Croatia). The lighthouse at Hvar and the archaeological museums at Nin (*Aenona*, Croatia) and Zadar were also visited.

Figure 15. Sirmium, visited in 1961...

The main Congress then ran from 17 to 23 September with delegates continuing to travel around. The Congress was officially opened in Celje (*Celeia,* Slovenia) with lectures given there and in Ptuj (*Poetovio,* Slovenia), Zagreb (Croatia), Osijek (*Mursa,* Croatia), Sremska Mitrovica (*Sirmium,* Serbia) and Belgrade (*Singidunum*). It must have been quite an exhausting itinerary. Museums were visited in many towns. Other visits included the mithraeum in Ptuj (*Poetovio*) and the Roman remains at Osijek (*Mursa*). The closing ceremony was held in Beograd (Belgrade, *Singidunum,* Serbia).

The pace was maintained during the post-Congress excursion to Upper Moesia. The Congress travelled along the Danube by steamer through the Iron Gates visiting the museum at Prahovo. Gamzigrad and Niš (*Naissus,* Serbia) occupied the second day with *Justiniana Prima* and the archaeological remains at Skopje and Stobi (North Macedonia) following on the final two days (some of these sites were again visited during the Serbian Congress in 2018, Figure 15).

The Congress was well looked after by the local and provincial authorities with many receptions offered by them and the main archaeological institutions including the Yugoslav Academy of Sciences and Arts and provincial academies (Figure 16). John Wilkes, who visited the Congress because he was completing his PhD on Dalmatia, reported that one of the organisers always carried a Gladstone bag and this contained

... and in 2018

Figure 16. Group photo of participants during the visit to Ptuj

the cash with which he paid for the meals and refreshments taken by the participants on their journeys.

There was only a slight reduction in numbers from the large volume of participants seen in Durham two years earlier, with 70 participants (plus an additional 14 partners or children) from 16 countries (Algeria, Austria, Belgium, Bulgaria, Czechoslovakia, France, Germany, Greece, Italy, Israel, the Netherlands, Poland, Switzerland, Yugoslavia, the UK and the USA). Many were regular participants, but they were joined by others who would subsequently make their names in Roman army or frontier studies including Titus Kolnik, Miroslava Mirković, Jaroslav Šašel and Graham Webster. Many archaeologists from Yugoslavia took the opportunity of a congress in their country to attend, with 28% of the delegates coming from the host country. Most of the papers were on the frontier in Europe but Mordechai Gichon spoke on Arabia and Jean Baradez on Numidia. Nineteen papers were published in three languages – English, German and French – these three became the standard languages for all future congresses.

Publication

Novak, G. (ed.) 1963. *Quintus congressus internationalis limitis Romani studiosorum, Diebus 17-23 Septembris anni 1961.* Zagreb: Jugoslavenska akademija znanosti i umjenosti.

The Sixth Congress, Arnoldshain, Germany 1964

The Congress took place in Germany close to the Upper German limes in the Roman province of Germania Superior from Tuesday 1 to Monday 7 September 1964. After two and a half days of lectures, the participants started on Friday September 4 on an excursion that first took them by coach along the Upper German and Raetian Limes to Eichstätt on the Danube. From here the route followed the river-frontier to Regensburg by ship, where, after further lectures, the final session of the Congress took place.

The Congress was organised by Hans Schönberger, Director of Saalburg Museum, and based at Arnoldshain in the Taunus, 15 km north-west of Bad Homburg. The location of the Congress was the Evangelical Academy in Arnoldshain, where most of the participants were also accommodated (Figure 17). The number of participants had risen to exactly one hundred from Austria, Belgium, Bulgaria, Czechoslovakia, France, Hungary, Israel, Italy, the Netherlands, Switzerland and the UK. These included 13 women, of which three gave lectures, Lady Aileen Fox from Exeter, Elisabeth Ettlinger from Zürich and Grace Simpson from Oxford within an environment still strongly dominated by men. The active participation of *limes* researchers from south-eastern Europe was remarkable: Radu Florescu and Emil Condurachi, Bucharest (Figure 18); Jenő Fitz, Székesfehérvár; Theofil Ivanov, Sofia; Frantisek Krizek, Brno; András Mócsy

Figure 17. The Evangelical Academy in Arnoldshain

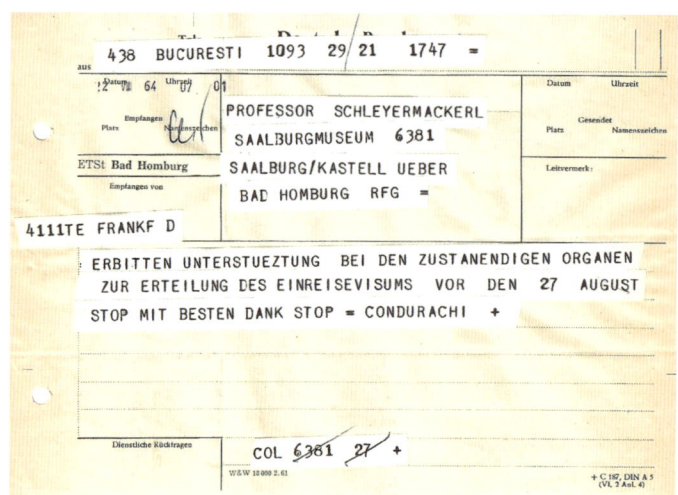

Figure 18. Telegram from Prof Emil Condurachi from Bucharest asking for an entrance visa.

and Sándor Soproni, Budapest; Esad Pašalić, Sarajevo; and Peter Petru, Ljubljana. Some combined their trip with a visit to the Römisch-Germanische Kommission in nearby Frankfurt. A number of participants were now Congress regulars, others attending for the first time, including young researchers who were to make important contributions to the development of provincial Roman archaeology as an independent

Figure 19. Albert van Giffen (with the back to the camera) talking to Maurice Euzennat(?). Behind them is Arend Hubrecht, who would later become director of Kam Museum in Nijmegen

field of study in Germany and elsewhere in the following years, like Dietwulf Baatz, Hans-Ulrich Nuber, Günter Ulbert and Arend Hubrecht (Figure 19). A local newspaper *Der Taunusbote* published a small report about the Congress for the general public (Figure 20).

In the afternoon of the second day, there was a visit to Saalburg to see the Roman fort, museum and reconstructions and the nearby remains of the frontier, and the next afternoon there was an excursion to excavations at the Augustan site of Rödgen.

After the lectures had concluded most participants led by Hans Schönberger visited a range of sites on their excursion to Regensburg. These included the *numeruskastell* at Würzberg and the fort at Oberscheidental along the Odenwald *limes*, the *limes* at Haghof, Aalen, Oberdorf am Ipf, the Raetian wall at Petersbuch, Pfünz, Pförring, the eastern end of the Raetian wall, Eining and finally the legionary fortress at Regensburg.

Figure 20. Communication at Arnoldshain was by letter and telegram (see Figure 18), though press interest was the same as today. On the newspaper cutting, from the left, are Professor Schütte and Eric Birley with Hans Schönberger behind

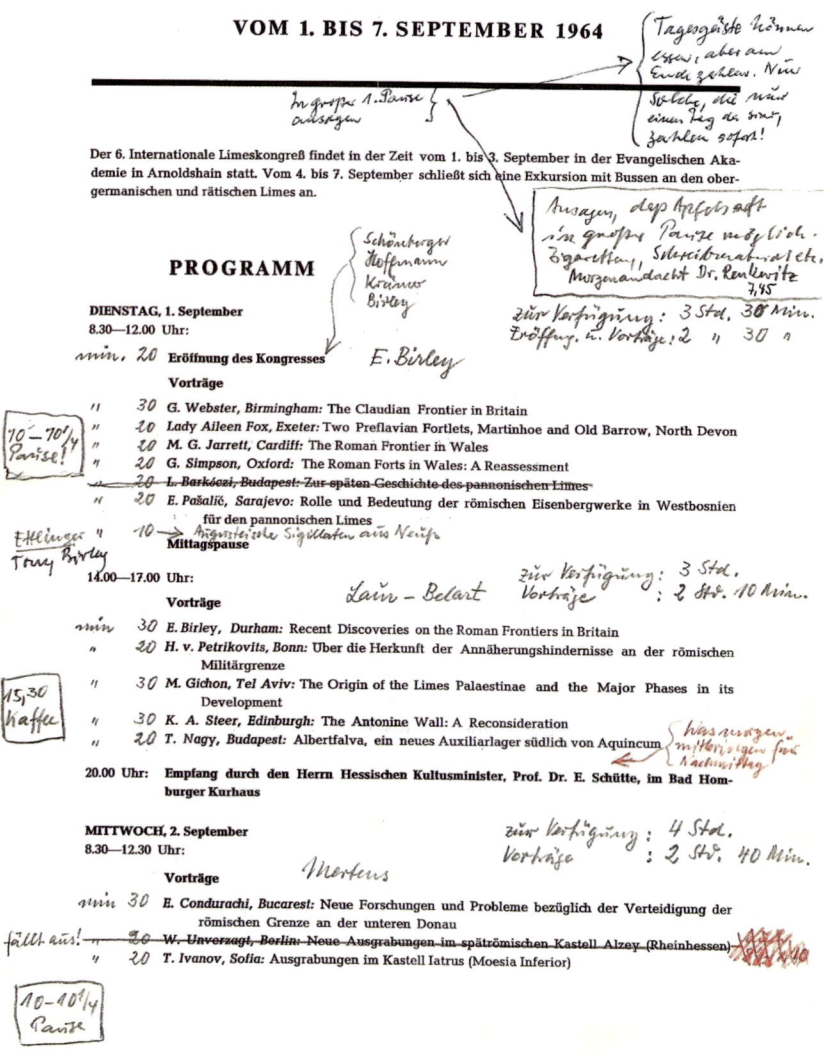

Figure 21. Schönberger's hand-written copy of the repeatedly changed and supplemented Arnoldshain lecture program

Twenty-seven papers were published in the now usual three languages. This was the first of the three volumes to be entitled *Studien zu den Militärgrenzen Roms*. The papers were mainly focussed on Europe but included Jean Baradez on the *Fossatum Africae* and Maurice Euzennat on the *limes* at Volubilis in Mauretania Tingitana, as well as Mordechai Gichon on the *limes Palaestinae* (Figure 21).

Publication

[Schönberger, H (ed.)] 1967. *Studien zu den Militärgrenzen Roms. Vorträge des 6. Internationalen Limeskongresses in Süddeutschland.* Köln: Bonner Jahrbücher Beihefte 19.

Demougeot, É. 1968. 'Review of *Studien ...*', in *Revue des études ancienne* 70 (1): 243-8.

Saria, B. 1968. 'Review of *Studien ...*', in *Südost Forschungen* 27: 384-5.

Liebmann-Frankfort, T. 1969. 'Review of *Studien ...*', in *Latomus* 28 (1): 287-9.

Reminiscences

Jeff Davies (UK)

My first Limes Congress was both an enormously exciting and awesome experience. Having graduated that summer, I was privileged to be conveyed to what was to be my first international conference as a passenger in Professor Mike Jarrett's MGB, driving from Cardiff to Lydd Ferryfield (airport) where we first flew in a Bristol Boxcar to Ostend and thence at high speed to Arnoldshain in the Taunus. I must confess that elements of the lecture programme were unfortunately unintelligible due to my lack of German, although I much enjoyed the guided excursions and the post-Congress tour, though as a poor student I did not participate in the three day cruise on the Danube to Regensburg. The sites visited were exciting by virtue of novelty such as the bank and ditch and stone watch-towers of the Upper German *limes* among the trees of the Taunus; the extent of excavations at forts such as Aalen, where a brand-new museum had been built on the site; or restoration, as at the never-to-be-forgotten Saalburg where Dietwulf Baatz expounded upon his practical research into *ballistae*. The numerous official receptions were also a high point where liquid refreshment facilitated my introduction to the 'big beasts' of Roman military scholarship such as Professor Eric Birley who deigned to speak to a lowly student, as well as individuals such as Jochen Garbsch whose friendship was reinforced at subsequent Congresses. As an intended co-driver of the Cardiff University Departmental Land Rover, I was looking forward to the next Congress in Israel but, alas, had to eschew the opportunity at the last minute. The vehicle was badly damaged in a crash in Syria.

John Peter Wild (UK)

My First Congress was Arnoldshain, attended at the end of a year in Bonn. I returned to Germany in 1974 where I shared a bed with Stephen Johnson at a bed-and-breakfast in Xanten where the organisers had billeted us. My paper, delivered in German, was on a pottery kiln we had been excavating at Longthorpe in the hope of obtaining information on parallels, but in vain. Most of the Anglophones walked out as I stood up to speak!

The Seventh Congress, Tel Aviv, Israel 1967

The Congress was held at Tel Aviv University in the Roman province of Syria Palaestina from Wednesday 3 to Monday 8 April and was followed by an extensive post-Congress tour lasting until Saturday 15 April.

This Congress was held outside Europe for the first time, travelling to Israel at the initiative of Mordechai Gichon (Figure 22). Supporters included the Ministry of Education, the Department of Antiquities and Museums, the Israel Defence Forces, the Mayors of Tel Aviv, Jerusalem, Beersheba and Acra, the Israel Museum, the Museum Haaretz, the Acre Museum, the Jaffa Museum of Antiquities, the National Parks Authority, the Israel Exploration Society, the Hebrew University, Jerusalem, and the Zionist Federation of Great Britain and Ireland, with several bodies hosting receptions for the Congress.

About 84 participants, several with partners, attended the Congress from 16 countries: Austria, Belgium, Bulgaria, Canada, Czechoslovakia, France, Germany, Greece, Hungary, Italy, the Netherlands, Romania, Switzerland, the UK, USA and Yugoslavia.

The lecture sessions were held in Tel Aviv University, where the Rector hosted lunch and the head of the Department of History a reception, and at Beersheba to the south. The places visited in this phase of the Congress included the excavations at Caesarea, 'Athlit, 'Ein Boqeq, 'Avdat and Mempsis, the fort at Tamara, Beersheba Museum, Haaretz Museum (now the Eretz Israel Museum) in Tel Aviv, Jaffa Museum, and Masada where excavations had recently taken place. The Congress then proceeded to Jerusalem where the Hebrew University, the Israel Exploration Society and the Israel Museum hosted a reception and the Deputy-Minister of Education and Culture and the Mayor of Jerusalem dinner. There were visits to the Israel Museum, the excavations at Megido, Beth Alphas Synagogue, and the Roman theatre and museum at Beth Shean. The final tours were to the synagogue at Capernaum, Heptapegon and Nazareth, amongst other sites and excavations, with the closing session held in the Hall of the Knight of St. John in Acre. Forty-two papers were read and 37 of these were published in the usual three languages. As well as the normal range of papers from Europe, including late Roman lectures, there were a significant number from Israel, presenting on a range of relevant archaeological topics from the area (Figures 23 and 24).

The Acta were edited by Shimon Applebaum, Professor of Classical Archaeology and Jewish History at the University of Tel Aviv, who had been present at the First Congress 18 years earlier, and contained an obituary of Jean Baradez who had died between the Congress and the publication of its proceedings.

Figure 22. Mordechai Gichon's formal invitation letter to host the next Congress in Tel Aviv.

Publication

Applebaum, S. (ed.) 1971. *Roman Frontier Studies, 1967. The Proceedings of the Seventh international Congress held at Tel Aviv*. Tel Aviv: Students' Organisation of Tel Aviv University.

Negev, A. 1975. 'Review of *Roman Frontier Studies, 1967*', in *Israel Exploration Society* 25: 51-3.

Figure 23. The 'high table' at the Congress in Tel Aviv. From the left, unknown, Jules Bogaers, unknown, unknown, Rudolf Laur-Belart, C.E. Stevens, Mordechai Gichon.

Figure 24. Congress participants attending a lecture in Israel in 1967 (note the smoking in the auditorium). Among those present were: left of the aisle, second row, Barri Jones; right of the aisle, second row, second Hans Schönberger, third John Gillam, fifth John Mann, sixth Teofil Ivanov; third row, first Michael Jarrett, second Dorothy Charlesworth, seventh Dietwulf Baatz

The Eighth Congress, Cardiff, Wales, UK 1969

The Congress ran from Thursday 28 August to Sunday 7 September in Wales in the Roman province of Britannia. It was preceded by a tour of southern England from Monday 25 to Thursday 28 September. As was by now customary for the British Congresses, it linked in with the Pilgrimage of Hadrian's Wall which followed the Congress from Sunday 7 to Friday 12 September.

The Congress was sponsored by the University of Wales and the University of Birmingham with Michael Jarrett (University College, Cardiff) and Graham Webster (University of Birmingham) the main organisers. The cost of attendance was £40 = $96.

The pre-Congress tour was led by Sheppard Frere and Edith Wightman (who was tragically murdered in her office in 1983), visits including the Saxon Shore forts at Richborough (*Rutupiae*), Lympne (*Portus Lemanis*), Pevensey (*Anderitum*) and Portchester (*Portus Adurni*), Fishbourne Roman Palace, Badbury Rings, Hod Hill and Bath (*Aquae Sulis*).

Attendance stood at 96 with several participants accompanied by their spouse, one by a child. Most of the lectures were delivered in Cardiff, with others in Coventry and Birmingham. Tours during the Congress whilst based in Cardiff included Cardiff fort, Neath Roman fort together with two practice camps at Loughor, Blaen-cwm-bach camp, Coelbren fort, Brecon Gaer fort (Figure 25), Caerwent Roman town, Caerleon legionary fortress, Newport Museum, Lydney Park Roman temples, the excavations at the fort at Usk (Figure 26), Cirencester Museum, Coventry Museum, and The Lunt where the partially reconstructed fort was inspected. Delegates then moved north to visit Wroxeter Roman city, Old Oswestry hill fort, Chester (including the Grosvenor Museum), Caernarfon fort and Tomen-y-Mur fort, with the final two days occupied by visits to York, including the newly discovered legionary headquarters building below York Minster, and the Yorkshire Museum. The closing session, arranged by Peter Wenham, took place in St John's College, York.

The Congress was treated to receptions by the Lord Mayor of Cardiff, the University of Wales, the National Museum of Wales, the Lord Mayor of Coventry, the Mayor of Chester, and the University of Birmingham.

After the Congress, many members took part in the Pilgrimage of Hadrian's Wall, beginning on the evening of Sunday 7 September. En route to Newcastle the group visited Durham Cathedral, stopping for lunch in a motorway car-park. Michael Jarrett

Figure 25. The visit to the fort at Brecon Gaer during the Welsh Congress. John Mann is to the left holding paper, Harald von Petrikovits to the right

had made arrangements for lunch to be carried on the coach (including soup in an urn) but the manager of the service station looked on this with displeasure and evicted the Congress from the coach park.

Michael Jarrett published the second edition of V.E. Nash-Williams, *The Roman Frontier in Wales* (Cardiff 1969), to coincide with the Congress. The proceedings were published by Eric Birley, Brian Dobson and Michael Jarrett and included 32 papers in the usual three languages. Four papers on general themes were followed by papers on Wales and the Marches and the remainder arranged geographically starting with Britain and then proceeding round the Empire in clockwise order. The volume was dedicated to the memory of Jean Baradez and includes a twenty-year review of previous Congresses by Eric Birley.

Publication

Birley, E., Dobson, B. and Jarrett, M.G. (eds) 1974. *Roman Frontier Studies, 1969. Eighth International Congress of* Limesforschung. Cardiff: University of Wales Press.

Nash-Williams, V.E 1969. *The Roman Frontier in Wales,* 2nd, revised, edition by Michael G. Jarrett, Cardiff: University of Wales Press.

Figure 26. Visiting the excavations at Usk in South Wales

Boon, G.C. 1975. 'Review of *Roman Frontier Studies 1969*', in *Archaeologia Cambrensis* 124: 117.
Todd, M. 1976. 'Review of *Roman Frontier Studies 1969*', in *Germania* 54 (1): 247.
Webster, G. 1976. 'Review of *Roman Frontier Studies 1969*', in *Britannia* 7: 393-4.

Reminiscence

David Breeze (UK)

This was my First Congress. I remember travelling down to Cardiff from Durham with Brian Dobson, John Gillam and John Mann, and meeting Gordon Maxwell [from Scotland] for the first time on that train. I learnt several important lessons at that Congress. To my amazement, the very eminent Dutch archaeologist Jules Bogaers came to talk to me, a mere post grad, about a paper I had just published, revealing his greatness of spirit and teaching me about one value of the Congress, a forum for discussion between the learned and the novice. My professor was not enamoured with my paper delivered in Cardiff but Hans Schönberger spoke to me afterwards and offered me encouragement to continue with the research; who could fail to be cheered by support from the First Director of the Römisch-Germanische Kommission, another great-hearted man. It was good to reminisce with his son and daughter-in-law at Siegmar von Schnurbein's retirement in Frankfurt 40 years later. But there were other lessons. No one had checked out a particular route pretending to be a 57-seater coach and so we got stuck on a bend on a narrow road … sitting in a new coach specially bought for the occasion. And I discovered that a 4-hour long journey to admire a field in which we were told once sat a Roman fort was not a good idea. As Carol van Driel-Murray later remarked, 'I now understand your near-obsessive preoccupation with the preparations for excursions'.

The Ninth Congress, Mamaïa, Romania 1972

The Congress was hosted in the holiday resort of Mamaïa on the northern outskirts of Constanța in the Roman province of Moesia Inferior from Wednesday 6 to Wednesday 13 September 1972. The post-Congress tour, from Thursday 14 to 17 September, was held in Transylvania, that is, Roman Dacia.

The invitation to hold the Congress in Romania was issued by the Romanian historian and archaeologist Emil Condurachi. It was expected that the Congress would be held in Dacia, but it was located in the Black Sea resort of Mamaïa in Lower Moesia. The language of the Congress organisation was French. There was a large increase in the number of participants – some 177 in total – meaning that there were so many papers offered (69), that there were two parallel sessions for the first time; these were held on the latter two of the four days of lectures, one session on archaeology and the other on history. On one notable day, the British archaeologist and pottery specialist J.P. Gillam met his namesake, the eminent American papyrologist and student of the Roman army J.P. Gilliam of the USA at a lecture for the first (and only) time. The days of lectures were usually followed by films each evening on the archaeology of Romania.

The location of the Congress in the region of the Dobruja, confined between the Danube and the Black Sea in the south-east corner of Romania, resulted in all the tours being restricted to that area. Visits were made to the Greek cities on the Black Sea coast, Constanța, Mangalia (*Callatis*) and Histria as well as the late Roman forts along the river. One highlight was the visit to the *Tropaeum Traiani* monument at Adamklissi. This was before it had been restored and the metopes placed in its present museum. The last two days of the Congress consisted of a tour along the Danube, partly by ship (a vessel appropriately named *Decebal*, after the Dacian king, was passed on the voyage – Figure 27), staying overnight at Brăila beside the point where the Danube turns east and the delta begins. En route, the great Roman forts of Cappidava (Figure 28) and Carsium were visited and the legionary base of Troesmis passed. The following day started with a visit to the most northerly fort in Lower Moesia, Dinogetia, on an island in the Danube to which the Congress was ferried (Figure 29).

The post-Congress tour started on Thursday 14 September with the participants journeying by train from Constanța to Cluj-Napoca. Pausing in Bucharest, some delegates visited the legendary Romanian archaeologist Constantine Diacoviciu in his study; his son Hadrian Diacoviciu was a delegate on the Congress. It was a small group who then set out to explore the frontier in Dacia, travelling over the following three days in a single coach. Forts and museums visited included Bologa, Buciumi,

Figure 27. The paddle steamer *Decebal* passed on the Danube

Figure 28. The late Roman fort at Cappidava

Figure 29. Congress participants on a ferry to visit Dinogetia

Romanaș, Zalău, Alba Iulia and Deva as well as *Sarmizegutusa* and the Dacian fortress at Costeşti. Travelling northwards through the Olt valley and then visiting forts on the edge of the Carpathians gave the participants in this tour an excellent introduction to the geography of Dacia. The tour returned to Bucharest on 17 September. The proceedings were edited by the Director of the Archaeological Institute of Bucharest, Dionisie Pippidi, and contained 57 papers in the usual three languages.

Publication

Pippidi, D.M. (ed.) 1974. *Actes du XIe congrès international d'études sur les frontières Romaines, Mamaïa, 6-13 Septembre 1972*. Bucureşti: Academiei Bucuresti Romania.

Reminiscence

David Breeze (UK)

Missing from the itineraries was a visit to the *Valu lui Traian* presumably because it was then generally not considered to be Roman in date. Nevertheless, an intrepid group – Christoph Rüger (Germany) with Charles and Miriam Daniels, Barri Jones and myself (all UK) – skipped lectures one day and travelled across the Dobruja as far as Cernovadă inspecting the earthworks en route. Unfortunately, at Cernovadă photographing the remains, which happened to include a modern watch-tower, alerted the authorities to the presence of the group who were then arrested by sailors on a tractor and taken to the local police station where the film in the cameras was confiscated, apart, that is, from Charles Daniels' film as he had removed it as soon as the sailors appeared and placed it under the front seat of his car. Christoph Rüger was the most nonchalant about the arrest, shrugging his shoulders and saying, 'this has happened to me before'.

The Tenth Congress, Xanten and Nijmegen, Germany and the Netherlands 1974

The Congress took place in the province of Germania Inferior (Lower Germany) from Friday 13 to Thursday 19 September. The base of the Congress for many participants was a ship moored at Xanten on the Rhine. The Congress moved to Nijmegen for the last day. A pre-Congress tour visited forts on the Rhine from Mainz to Xanten from Tuesday 10 to Friday 13 September. The post-Congress tour explored sites in the Netherlands from Friday 20 to Monday 23 September.

The organising committee was formed of Joseph Mertens from Belgium, Jules Bogaers of the Netherlands (Figure 30) together with Harald von Petrikovits and Hans Schönberger of Germany. There was again a large number of participants, numbering about 180. Sixty-eight papers were given in three languages (English, German and French) supplemented by 14 introductory lectures on the site visits. There were two days of lectures in Xanten and half a day in Nijmegen.

A special exhibition in Xanten featured Roman helmets from Lower Germany. Visits took place to Asberg, Gellep and Alpen; Cologne; Xanten (Figure 31) and Vetera;

Figure 30. Jules Bogaers, one of the organisers of the 1974 Congress

Figure 31. Visiting an excavation at Xanten (note the attire)

Figure 32. Harald von Petrikovits examining a section at Haltern in 1974

Figure 33. Participants returning to the hotel ship moored at Xanten

with the delegates offered a choice between the excavations at the legionary base at Haltern (Figure 32) where they inspected the excavations of Siegmar von Schnurbein, and also visited Tongeren (the Roman town of *Aduatuca Tungrorum*) on the last day. After six days in Xanten, the Congress moved to Nijmegen, guided through the Arnhem battlefield by Arend Hubrecht, onto where the last day of lectures was held. Here a reception was given by the Municipality of Nijmegen in the town hall hosted by the mayor of the town.

The pre-Congress excursion ran over four days from Tuesday 10 to Friday 13 September. It started in Mainz with a visit to the Römisch-Germanisches Zentralmuseum. On the quay adjacent to the museum, the M.S. Rijnstroom awaited the participants in the expedition (Figure 33). This transported the group down river to Xanten, stopping at Roman sites and museums along the way. These included Boppard (where the mayor offered a reception and wine tasting), Koblenz and the great Prussian fortress of Ehrenbreitstein overlooking the confluences of the rivers Rhine and Mosel, the tower at Bad Hönningen and the adjacent *limes*, Remagen and Bonn.

The post-Congress excursion ran from Friday 20 to Monday 23 September. Following introductory lectures on Nijmegen, the excavations in the town and the G.M. Kam Museum were visited (Figures 34, 35 and 36). Delegates were offered a choice between the Gallo-Roman temple at Elst or the town of Utrecht in the morning, succeeded by a visit to Amersfoort and Zwammerdam. The excavations at Valkenburg and Velsen were also seen as well as the National Museum in Leiden and the Institute of Pre- and Proto-History in Amsterdam.

A special handbook to the frontier in Lower Germany was produced to coincide with the Congress. At the Congress, Eric Birley, who was unable to attend, was acclaimed

A History of the Congress of Roman Frontier Studies 1949-2024

Figure 34. The Congress welcomed to the G.M. Kam Museum in Nijmegen by Arend Hubrecht

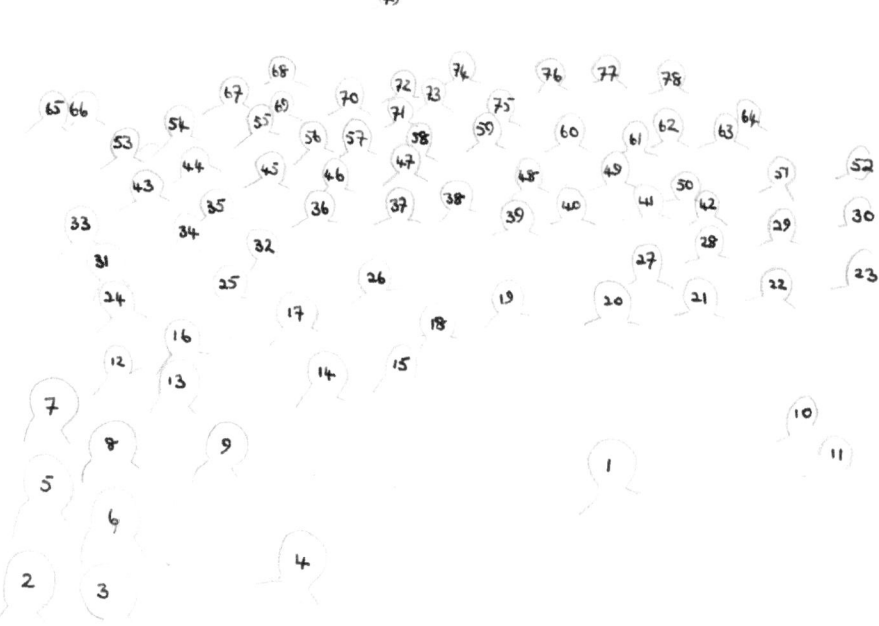

1. Hubrecht
2.
3. Rivet
4. Alföldy
5.
6. Doppelfeld
7. Johnson
8. Rüger
9. Wachtel
10.
11.
12. Robertson
13. Ubl
14. Breeze
15. Dobson
16. Ubl
17. Harper
18. Maxfield
19.
20. Daniels
21.
22.
23. Petrikovits
24. Brulet
25. Liebeschuetz
26. Mann
27. Ivanov
28. Sasel
29.
30.
31.
32. Baatz
33. Wright
34. Roller
35. Mócsy
36. Hellenkemper
37. Soproni
38. Hubrecht
39. Miss Hubrecht
40. Miss Hubrecht
41. Gablet
42. Brunsting
43. Hobley
44. Swan
45. Fitz
46. Scott
47. Bouchenaki
48.
49. Beckmann
50. Beckmann
51. Gichon
52. Schoppa
53. Manning
54. Gillam
55. Moore
56.
57. Gracey
58.
59.
60. Hassall
61. Daniels
62. Paar
63. Eames
64.
65. Smeesters
66.
67. Mertens
68. Thijssen
69.
70. Raepsaet
71. Raepsaet
72. Horn
73. Bloemers
74. Burger
75. Sarfatij
76.
77.
78. Pocsy?
79.

Figure 35. Names of people identified in Figure 34

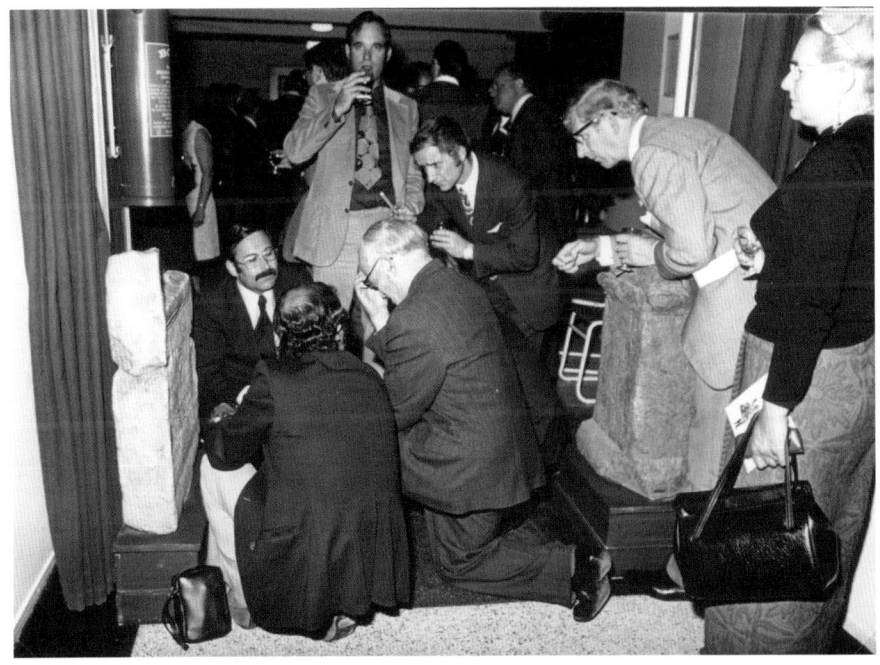

Figure 36. Epigraphists at work – a relatively common sight at a Limes Congress, Christoph Rüger and Richard Wright on their knees with Donald Moore, leaning on an altar, and, in the back, Martin Hartmann with a glass, in the museum at Nijmegen.

honorary president for life and the Congress proceedings were dedicated to his 70th birthday. The proceedings were published in 1977, organised by province with a short section on general topics at the end, and concluded with perhaps the most detailed index of any Congress proceedings.

Publications

Haupt, D. and Horn, H.G. (eds) 1977. *Studien zu den Militärgrenzen Roms, II. Vorträge des 10. Internationalen Limeskongresses in der Germania Inferior*. Köln: Bonner Jahrbücher Beihefte 38.

Bogaers, J.E. and Rüger, C.B. (eds) 1974. *Der Niedergermanische Limes*. Bonn: Rudolf Habelt.

Reminiscences

Raymond Brulet (Belgium)

Un congrès au fil de l'eau …

It was a Tuesday in September, I was approaching the Rhine from the station with a heavy suitcase. The boat was on the Rhine bank from noon in the immediate neighbourhood of the Römisch-Germanisches Zentralmuseum in Mainz. This was the welcome day for the participants of the pre-Congress Tour of the X Internationaal Limes-Congress which will take place in Lower Germany, Xanten and Nijmegen.

I am overwhelmed with nervousness and curiosity, especially because the river view is attractive and because I am arriving at my first Limes Congress. The surprise is complete, the first delegates are accommodated on board a Dutch hotel boat for ten days, until the start of the post-Congress excursion in the Netherlands (Figure 33). Whether for excursions or work sessions, participants leave the ship, buses awaiting them each time at different site locations to which it has sailed, to be transported to the visits and the lectures. A Congress along the water…! Full of interest and good times.

The next day the boat left Mainz for Boppard and on the third day we had the opportunity to stop in Koblenz, then in Remagen with the impressive visit of the *caput limitis* opposite Vinxtbach.

Throughout the official duration of the Congress, between Xanten and Nijmegen, the participants accommodated on board returned tired and satisfied to their sleeper cabins, rocked by the waves and the sounds of the great river. But one of the richest aspects of this river adventure is the fact that, in the evening, the archaeologists were close to each other and met at the bar of the boat to discuss their projects and above all to offer a few toasts to the future. An extraordinary experience and great convivial moments which brought us all closer together.

Zsolt Visy (Hungary)

The Congress was organised in Xanten by Christoph B. Rüger in 1974, with two additional days in the Netherlands. Our group was greeted by the mayor of Nijmegen in front of the museum with the following words: 'warm greetings to the Germans who now came by buses and not by tanks'. Because of my financial situation, I travelled by a Jawa motorcycle, as some colleagues remembered at later conferences.

It was my first Limes Congress. That time I had been working for five years in the cemetery and vicus of *Intercisa* (Dunaújváros); thus it was interesting to see and study other methods applied in Xanten, in Miltenberg and in *Asciburgium*, and admire the perfect presentation by Dieter Planck about the Dalkingen Gate. We listened to a very good lecture by W. van Es in Utrecht about Roman archaeological research in the Netherlands. The new archaeological exhibition was opened in Cologne. It made a huge impression not only on me but, as I could see, also on the other Congress participants.

I met and consulted with many famous scholars both in Xanten and Nijmegen like Professors Eric Birley, H. von Petrikovits, S.S. Frere, J. Mertens, M. Euzennat and others for the first time. I will also mention the important novelty of this Congress. It was the first time that a booklet was prepared and edited about the *limes* sites of the territory in question by C.B. Rüger and J.E. Bogaers. This good example was followed by the organisers of later conferences.

The Eleventh Congress, Székesfehérvár, Hungary 1976

The Congress took place in Székesfehérvár, Dunaújváros and Budapest in the Roman province of Pannonia Inferior from Monday 30 August to Monday 6 September 1976. The pre-Congress tour ran from Thursday 26 to Sunday 29 August visiting sites along the Danube in eastern Austria and western Hungary. The post-Congress tour, from Tuesday 7 to Thursday 9 September, was focussed on the Danube south of Budapest.

For the Eleventh Congress, the venue moved from the Rhine to the Danube and there were 156 participants. The Congress opened in Székesfehérvár where the delegates were based. Here, the King Stephen Museum had created a special exhibition on the 'Plastic art of the Roman era in Pannonia', and hosted a reception on the first evening, following which there was an introduction to the tour the next day, the latter setting a pattern for the Congress. The three days of lectures were interspersed with tours, usually departing at 08.00. These were to the late Roman fortified settlement at Környe, Domokos Kuny museum and *lapidarium*, the fort at Nyergesújfalu, the fortress at Komárom-Esztergom, and the late fort at Tokod (Figure 37); the Roman town of *Gorsium*; Szentendre the fort and *lapidarium* at *Ulcisia Castra*, the late towers at Leányvár, Leányfalu, Visegrád (Figure

Figure 37. The fort of Tokod being inspected in 1976

Figure 38. The Valentinianic watch-tower at Steinbruch, Visegrád, with Eric Birley puffing on his pipe

38) and Dunabogdány, and the late forts at Visegrád, Pilismarót and Hidegletőskereszt; auxiliary forts *Intercisa* (Dunaujváros) and *Annamatia* (Baracs); the fort at *Campona* (Nagytétény), the archaeological park and other remains at *Aquincum* (Figure 39) and the National Museum in Budapest as well as other sites. A highlight was a concert at the Budenz House in Székesfehérvár at which music by Bela Bartok was played.

A pre-Congress excursion ran from Thursday 26 to Sunday 29 August starting in Carnuntum in Austria where delegates visited the museum and monuments (including the Heidentor – Figure 40) and the Government of Lower Austria hosted a reception. The tour then moved into Hungary, visiting Sopron (*Scarbantia*), Szombathely (*Savaria*), Keszthely, Fenékpuszta, Tihany and Veszprém.

The post-Congress excursion ran from Tuesday 7 to Thursday 9 September, inspecting the frontier south of Budapest. These included the forts at *Lussonium* (Paks), *Lugio* and Kölked and the late Roman fortified settlement at Ságvár. The middle day was spent at Pécs. The tour also visited the open-air display at Mohács recently created to commemorate the battle there in 1526 when Louis II, king of Hungary, was defeated and killed by the Ottoman army led by the Sultan Suleiman the Magnificent.

The proceedings contained 57 papers in the usual three languages, organised by the geographical topic of their subject. Unfortunately, the lectures given by Hungarian

Figure 39. *Contra Aquincum*, now covered over, in Budapest

Figure 40. The Heidentor, visited on the pre-Congress tour of 1976
(it was again visited in 1986)

scholars on their sites during the visits were not able to be included with the result that there are few Hungarian papers in the volume.

Publication

Fitz, J. (ed.) 1977. *Akten des XI. Internationalen Limes Kongresses (Székesfehérvár 30.8.-6.9.1976)*. Budapest: Akadémiai Kiadó.

Reminiscence

Bill Hanson (UK)

This was my First Congress after taking up a post as a lecturer at Glasgow University only the year before. Slightly in awe of the famous names that surrounded me, I gave a paper that offered an historical context for two sites that I had been excavating during the previous two years. Since one of my primary foci was a rejection of the then long-held view that enclosures beneath certain forts on the Antonine Wall were remnants of an earlier, Agricolan, halt on the isthmus, this did not go down well with everyone in the audience, not least Professor Eric Birley. Much to my discomfort, the grand old man of Roman frontier studies announced at the end of my lecture that he would take me aside later and put me right. Fortunately, he did neither, though it was a less than entirely auspicious start to my *Limes* career.

This was also my first trip behind the Iron Curtain and my first visit to the Danube, both memorable events in their own right. It also set the pattern for all future Congresses, as I took every opportunity to look around the sites we were being shown and to try to appreciate them in their topographic context. I was always trying to find the best position to photograph them and was usually one of the last to return to the bus, waiting impatiently to get a picture that showed the site unencumbered by *Limes* participants. I remember seeing some raised eyebrows at Tokod as I climbed an adjacent pylon to get the height I needed to encapsulate as much as I could of the defences of this restored late Roman fort.

The Twelfth Congress, Stirling, Scotland, UK 1979

The Congress took place in Stirling in Scotland in Britannia from Saturday 1 to Sunday 9 September 1979. Continuing the tradition started in 1949, it linked in with the Pilgrimage of Hadrian's Wall which preceded it from Saturday 25 to Friday 31 August.

Planning for the Congress started five years in advance with the formal invitation presented to the 1976 Congress (Figure 41). The committee for organising the Congress included Gordon Maxwell, Lawrence Keppie, Bill Hanson, Helen Adamson and David Breeze. Each member was assigned a specific task: Gordon Maxwell took on general oversight and finances; Lawrence Keppie acted as the secretary, dealing with the invitations and correspondence; David Breeze looked after the tours; Bill Hanson the lectures; Helen Adamson was in charge of social events; with the final member a representative of Stirling University (Figure 42).

Figure 41. David Breeze offering the invitation to hold the next Congress in Scotland at the closing session in 1976; seated from the left, András Mócsy, Eric Birley and Jenő Fitz

Figure 42. Most of the core team for the Stirling Congress, from left, Gordon Maxwell, Stephen Johnson, Bill Hanson, David Breeze and Lawrence Keppie

The Congress opened with a reception for the around 164 participants in Stirling Castle hosted by Malcolm Rifkind MP, the Minister for Home Affairs and the Environment at the Scottish Office. The following day the lecture programme started with four talks each providing background on the late prehistoric, Roman and early medieval periods in Scotland. They were succeeded by a series of nine lectures on recent work in different provinces of the Roman Empire; the intention of these lectures was to provide overviews that were otherwise lacking in the geographical sessions. Three days of lectures followed, three sessions running concurrently each day. Each delegate was issued with a booklet of lecture summaries. On the second evening there was a public lecture by Kenneth St Joseph from Cambridge University on 'Aerial Reconnaissance and the map of Roman Scotland' accompanied by an exhibition of his photographs.

Guiding on the tours was undertaken in three languages. Brian Dobson and Stephen Johnson led the German-speaking groups, Richard Reece the French, with Valerie Maxfield and Bill Hanson the English.

The site visits were arranged chronologically; owing to the number of participants the coaches operated in pairs, each pair visiting the same places but in opposite order.

Figure 43. Visit to the watch-tower above Fendoch

The first day included the Iron Age hill-fort of Dunsinane (cf. Shakespeare's *Macbeth*), the Cleaven Dyke (now known to be a prehistoric earth-work but then thought to be Roman), the legionary base at Inchtuthil, and the watch-tower at Fendoch (Figure 43). During the second tour, the whole of the Congress spent the morning inspecting the camps, fort and annexe at Ardoch, with Kaims Castle fortlet and Parkneuk watch-tower on the Gask Ridge in the afternoon. Cramond Roman fort and the National Museum of Antiquities of Scotland in Edinburgh occupied an afternoon. A day was devoted to the Antonine Wall with the stretch from Watling Lodge to the fort Rough Castle walked and then the sector from Dullatur over Croy Hill and Bar Hill to Twechar; the fortlet at Duntocher (Figure 44) and the Iron Age broch at Torwood were also visited. That evening was occupied by an exhibition in Stirling Museum. The newly excavated bath-house at Bearsden (Figures 45 and 46) and the Hunterian Museum occupied an afternoon. The last day of visits took the Congress to Carpow legionary fortress (Figure 47), Dundee City Museum with its Roman inscriptions, Meigle Museum of Pictish stones and the Tealing Iron Age souterrain/earth-house.

Special exhibitions were held. That at the Hunterian Museum in Glasgow University was ready only five minutes before the Congress arrived, so Lawrence Keppie from the Hunterian gave an impromptu lecture on the main university building (a splendid

Figure 44. The visit to the fortlet at Duntocher on the Antonine Wall; Anne Robertson used plant pots to mark out the excavation

Figure 45. David Breeze explains the bath-house at Bearsden to the Congress, with the Provost and former Provost to his left

Figure 46. Bearsden again, now in German by Brian Dobson

Victorian edifice) for 15 minutes before the delegates trooped inside. The Smith Museum and Art Gallery in Stirling also arranged a special collection on the Romans in Stirlingshire for the Congress.

The cinema at the MacRobert Centre in Stirling University ran a series of films with a Roman theme and one evening lecture was cut in mid-flow, so that the delegates could all watch a film at the advertised time. One evening there was a different form of 'entertainment'. Several delegates asked what were these 'temporary camps' which we were intending to visit. It was realised that few outside Britain had ever seen a Roman camp, so an evening lecture was quickly organised. One extra-curricular activity was an evening at the Edinburgh Military Tattoo to see how real soldiers operated!

The pre-Congress tour was on Thursday 1 September and took the form of the drive from Carlisle, where the Pilgrimage of Hadrian's Wall had ended, to Stirling via Burnswark and Birrens (*Blatobulgium*). Alfie Truckell, curator of Dumfries Museum, brought several relevant objects to Burnswark to show to the group.

Figure 47. John Wilkes' excavation at the Severan legionary base at Carpow is inspected

The post-Congress tour was the return run from Stirling to Newcastle upon Tyne via Pennymuir Roman camps, Woden Law hillfort and High Rochester (*Bremenium*).

The Proceedings of the Congress were published within 12 months by British Archaeological Reports in three volumes which included 77 papers published in the usual three languages arranged by Roman province with a general section at the end.

Publications

Hanson, W.S. and Keppie, L.J.F. (eds) 1980. *Roman Frontier Studies 1979. Papers presented to the 12th International Congress of Roman Frontier Studies.* Oxford: British Archaeological Reports International Series 71.

Breeze, D.J. 1979. *Roman Scotland. A Guide to the Visible Remains.* Newcastle upon Tyne: Frank Graham.

Breeze, D.J. 1979. *Roman Scotland. Some Recent Excavations.* Edinburgh: Scottish Development Department.

Keppie, L.J.F. 1979. *Roman Distance Slabs from the Antonine Wall*. Glasgow: Hunterian Museum.

Dierkens, A. 1981. 'Review of Roman Frontier Studies, 1979', in *Latomus* 40 (4): 888-9.

Reminiscences

Tom Parker‡ (USA)

This was my first Limes Congress. One abiding memory was the films being shown in the evenings. One evening it was 'Sebastiane'. I was standing at the bar when I observed Eric Birley going into the cinema; ten minutes later he appeared beside me. 'But, professor, I have just seen you going into the film'. 'Yes', said Eric, 'I came out after the second flagellation'!

David Breeze (UK)

When the jobs were divided up in the run up to the Congress, I was pleased to receive the task of organising the tours. I had worked in Scotland for nigh-on 10 years and knew the sites I wanted to show to the Congress and moreover had experience of running archaeological tours with Brian Dobson. Indeed we did a complete dry-run prior to the Congress with our Roman frontiers group.

The first question was where to hold the Congress. Edinburgh and Glasgow vied for the honour, so we went to Stirling and the university proved to be a good choice. Exhibitions take a long time to organise, so planning started early. Even then, one did not happen and that at the Hunterian Museum in Glasgow University was completed as the Congress arrived.

Bill was in charge of lectures. I doubt if he heard one as he spent his time checking all was going well in the lecture theatres. He and the rest of the Congress were frustrated when Professor St Joseph went on for an hour and a half – his normal practice – in the evening. At the ceilidh on the last evening the comedian started making jokes about foreigners (honest); Bill went up and pulled the plug out of the microphone.

I chose Scottish Motor Transport coaches for the Congress because they had toilets on board. Two met us in Carlisle at the end of the Pilgrimage and it was when we got to Burnswark en route to Stirling and they negotiated the narrow roads that I knew we were in safe hands. On the first tour of the Congress, the four coaches lined up at the university and at 9'oclock one driver got out his watch and all four drivers got into their coaches and we were off. We did leave one delegate behind on one day (Nicholas Reed) and he caught us up by hiring a taxi. The timing, I was pleased to note, went well. On one day, the coach led by Brian returned to the university 15 minutes early. 'I think that we should sit on the coach for another 15 minutes', said

Hans Schönberger, 'to keep to Dr Breeze's otherwise impeccable timing'. I have no idea whether the toilets were well used or not as I drove around in my car, checking gates were open and so on (I had my departmental colleagues build a couple of stiles to ease access at two sites). At Rough Castle, we were bemused at Anne Robertson coming round us all during lunch.' I have designated Coach X as the toilet coach for ladies and Eric Birley has been posted to ensure that no men go in.' 'But Anne', I said, 'all coaches have toilets.' 'Oh, yes, I know', was the reply, 'but you have got to walk past all the men to get there'.

The Thirteenth Congress, Aalen, Germany 1983

The Congress was held in Aalen in the Roman province of Raetia from Sunday 18 to Sunday 25 September. The pre-Congress excursion, from Wednesday 14 to Saturday 17 September, started at Basel and visited sites in Switzerland. The post-Congress tour from Monday 26 to Tuesday 27 September was along the Raetian Limes to Passau.

The Congress in Aalen took place partially in and mostly right next to the fort of the *Ala II Flavia miliaria*, the largest auxiliary unit on the Raetian *limes*. The city of Aalen, the county Ostalbkreis and the Landesdenkmalamt Baden-Württemberg had invited the Congress and they turned out to be generous hosts. The idea to hold the Congress in Aalen went back to a visit of Sheppard Frere in the Ostalbkreis in autumn 1977, during which Dieter Planck, Günter Ulbert and Bernhard Hildebrand (county archivist), among others, presented current research results to him. Prominent figures of the Congress besides the mentioned were Hans Schönberger and Eric Birley. The latter gave an overview of *limes* research since Ernst Fabricius, highlighting the important role of the Limes Congresses in the development of scholarship and friendship (Birley 1986). Hans Schönberger gave a brief overview of the history of the Congress and, looking back on its positive development, emphasised: 'The International Limes Congress has no fixed organisational form and no statutes. Each inviting country could and can organize it in a way that suits its characteristics and possibilities'. The Congress coincided with the publication of a catalogue by Philipp Filtzinger of the *Limesmuseum Aalen* opened exactly two years before.

With this Congress, numbers rose to a different level of magnitude: 284 attended from 20 countries, including, as specifically mentioned in the Congress Acta, 48 scientists from Eastern Europe. The participants delivered 120 papers, 50% up on the previous Congress (Figure 48). The number of presentations only once fell below 100 again. The extremely high number of participants was not reached again before the Congress in León in Spain 20 years later. As a reference to the difficulties in international scientific exchange that still existed at that time, it should be mentioned that despite personal invitations sent out about 18 months earlier to colleagues in the then German Democratic Republic (GDR – East Germany), none of the seven invited scientists was able to attend 'for scheduling reasons'. According to the GDR view, the invitation should have been issued at least two years in advance!

The Congress opened with a ceremony in the Town Hall with speeches interleaved with music (Corelli and Bach). There followed a series of papers in two sessions of lectures – separated by the respective provinces – on recent work in different provinces. That evening the mayor gave a reception at the Limesmuseum. On Monday evening there was a visit in the monastery of Neresheim, where Abbot Norbert introduced the

The Thirteenth Congress, Aalen, Germany 1983

Figure 48. An attentive audience in Aalen, 1983. Fourth row, from the left, Géza Alföldy, Michael Speidel, Sonja Jilek, Herma Stiglitz; fifth row, second from left, Klára Póczy; to the right, third row back, Margaret Roxan, Valerie Maxfield and Willy Groenman-van Waateringe

participants to the details of the spirituality underlying the late Baroque building. As a highlight of the following reception in Ellwangen Castle the evening saw the premiere of the music piece 'Ala II Flavia – March of the Aalen Riders', composed especially for the Congress and performed by the miners band of Schwäbisches Hüttenwerke GmbH Wasseralfingen (Figure 49). Tours during the Congress included Heidenheim an der Brenz, Rainau-Buch, the tower at Mahdholz (Figure 50), and Dalkingen. A second tour embraced Schwäbisch Gmünd, Rotenbachtal, Haghof, Welzheim, Rötelsee (Figure 51), Murrhardt, Wachtturm bei Grab, Mainhardt, Öhringen, Osterburken, Hönehaus and Walldürn. The third excursion was to Theilenhofen, Gunzenhausen, Ellingen, Harlach and Weissenburg, where the new great cover over the bath-house was with no doubt the outstanding site – notwithstanding the remark of C.S. Sommer (see below). At one museum, we were greeted by a reception committee, assembled to honour Pierre Salama. At the end of the Second World War, Pierre had entered the town with his French troops and posted a guard at the museum to prevent it being looted. Nearly 40 years on, his thoughtful act was still remembered by the town.

The pre-Congress tour from Wednesday to Saturday started at Basel in Switzerland, where the tombstone of Erasmus was visited by some participants. Along the route,

Figure 49. Sheet music of the 'March of Ala Flavia II' composed and premiered especially for the Congress by the Miners' Band from Wasseralfingen

Figure 50. The timber tower at Mahdholz recently created, one of the many treats provided by the Denkmalpflege in Baden-Württemberg

The Thirteenth Congress, Aalen, Germany 1983

Figure 51. Margot Klee explains the fortlet at Welzheim, Rötelsee to the Congress

Dangstetten, Augst, the late Roman *limes* on the High Rhine, Vindonissa, Zurzach (Figure 52) and several places at the Upper Neckar, including Rottweil and Köngen, were visited. The two-day post-Congress excursion embraced Roman sites in the Danube valley in Bavaria, including Faimingen, Eining, Kelheim, Regensburg, Straubing and Passau and ended with a reception in Passau on Tuesday evening.

The papers were published in the usual three languages, arranged by Roman provinces with a general section at the end. It appeared just in time for the Carnuntum Congress and was dedicated to Eric Birley on his 80th birthday. It speaks for the open spirit of the Limes Congresses that the suggestion for this dedication came from Manfred Kandler of the Austrian Archaeological Institute.

This Congress was notable for the hospitality at every level, from the state of Baden-Württemberg to the mayors of the towns and villages which were visited and the museum directors. Mordechai Gichon judged, 'in my opinion, the Congress was successful in almost every respect. ... Critically, I would remark on the Congress that more lectures should be held on site, i.e. if the weather permits, in the open in front of the objects, i.e. even more visual instruction in the field'.

At the very end of that Congress, a few delegates met to consider the issue of an increasing focus on the details of excavations to the exclusion of general papers or overviews (see reminiscence by C.S. Sommer below). As a result, David Breeze agreed

Figure 52. The late Roman fort at Zurzach in the rain visited on the pre-Congress excursion

to organise a thematic session at the next Congress on the subject of the impact of the Roman army on the indigeneous populations of the frontier zones (Vetters and Kandler 1990: 83-160).

Publications

Landratsamt Ostalbkreis (ed.) 1983. *XIII. Internationaler Limeskongress Aalen 18. bis 25. September 1983.* Ein Bericht von Bernhard Hildebrand. Aalen.

Unz, C. (ed.) 1986. *Studien zu den Militärgrenzen Roms III. 13. Internationaler Limeskongress Aalen 1983.* Stuttgart: Forschungen und Berichte zur Vor- und Frühgeschichte in Baden-Württemberg 20.

Unz, C. (ed.) 1983. *Führer zu römischen Militäranlagen in Süddeutschland. Herausgegeben aus Anlass des 13. International Limeskongresses in Aalen 18. bis 25. September 1983.* Stuttgart: Landesdenkmalamt Baden-Württemberg.

Reminiscences

Carol van Driel-Murray (Netherlands)

My first Limes Conference was actually Stirling (1979), but that was an excuse to benefit from the Antonine Wall excursions, as I was hardly interested in things Roman at the

Figure 53. Mordechai Gichon and C. Sebastian Sommer in Aalen

time. By 1983 it was different: Wil (Willy) Groenman-van Waateringe, my supervisor and a keen Limes Congress participant, insisted I give a paper. My first, and on shoes at that. I was terrified. All the great men, familiar from their publications, lined up on the front row (lecture rooms were smaller and more intimidating then). And then at questions, Eric Birley slowly rose to his feet..... My (visible) horror turned into open shock as Eric announced how much he'd enjoyed this, referring to the recent finds at Vindolanda. Fortunately, the dominance of a few scholars has now gone, but I never felt discriminated against as a young, female researcher – perhaps my odd specialisation helped there (the leather lady from Amsterdam): I didn't encroach on the establishment. And the excursions, with local wine served at every fort, and a real ox-roast in a castle courtyard soon broke down barriers. At Aalen I met great friendliness and encouragement: the basis of the Roman Military Equipment Conferences was laid there, a sign of new approaches from a new generation with different goals. But as a newcomer, a word of appreciation from a scholar like Harald von Petrikovits is something you treasure for life.

C. Sebastian Sommer‡ (Germany)

Having just returned from a two-year scholarship at St. Antony's at Oxford with a MPhil (Oxon) in my pocket, studying Roman provinces with Sheppard S. Frere, the Aalen Congress was my First Congress, having not missed one since I am happy to say – and it changed the direction of my life (Figure 53). This is because Dieter Planck took me to the side over one coffee break pretending to be interested in my past and my intentions for the future, ending that talk with an offer of a five-year contract excavating at Ladenburg. What followed was a huge stomach ache on my side as my ideas had been to do a three or so years PhD with Günter Ulbert perhaps followed by a tour around the Mediterranean with a DAI travel-scholarship. Fortunately, Siegmar von Schnurbein (whom I had not met before) and Günter Ulbert caught me somehow in several long discussions, suggesting that I should do a speedy PhD from literature and start the contract a year later, as the excavation was not that urgent (later I learned that the whole thing was somehow set up, as the three were the prominent members of the Ladenburg-Commission where that idea had been discussed a few weeks before). And so I did – a PhD about the military vici of Upper Germany and Raetia and after a year the job in Ladenburg – but due to the following career in German heritage management I never saw the sites in North Africa and many other areas worthwhile visiting.

The other important memory of the Congress, besides an encouraging shoulder slap from Hans Schönberger after my first intervention in a debate after a lecture, is an amazing amount of very particular facts and details for a large number of sites particularly in Germany but elsewhere, too. This led to the 'classic' statement of David Breeze and a number of British and Dutch colleagues to be heard at many Congresses after very specialised lectures: "Not another second tepidarium of the baths of xyz".

The Fourteenth Congress, Carnuntum, Austria 1986

The Congress took place in Carnuntum in Austria (Pannonia Superior) from Sunday 14 to Sunday 21 September 1986. The pre-Congress tour along the Danube up-stream from Vienna ran from Wednesday 10 to Saturday 13 September, and the post-Congress tour to Slovakia from Monday 22 to Wednesday 24 September.

The main organisers of the Congress were Hermann Vetters (Figure 54) and Manfred Kandler. There were over 200 archaeologists and ancient historians from 21 European and overseas countries at the conference. The opening ceremony was held in the grand surroundings of the Castle of Traun in Petronell.

The total number of papers presented was 104 from around the Roman Empire. The opening two sections were on military history and the special theme was the

Figure 54. Hermann Vetters (left) with Eric Birley

Figure 55. Guiding by Herma Stiglitz

impact of the Roman army on the indigenous peoples chaired by Willy Groenman-van Waateringe.

Excursions during the Congress included a thorough inspection of Carnuntum and its excavations and museum. In Vienna, the Congress was welcomed to the city at the Akademie der Wissenschaften where an introductory lecture to the Roman remains was presented. The Kunsthistorisches Museum and the Historical Museum of the City of Vienna were visited. The following excursions were arranged thematically. The first was to the hinterland of Carnuntum, visiting the small fort at Höflein, the *villa rustica* at Bruckendorf, the museum at Eisenstadt, the *burgus* at Leithaprodersdorf, the museum at Mannersdorf and with lunch provided by the province of Burgenland. The next day the theme was 'Barbaricum' with visits to the prehistoric fortifications and Roman stations at Stillfried and Oberleis beyond the frontier.

The pre-Congress excursion started in Wels in Upper Austria, moving on to examine forts and towers along the Danube: Oberanna led by Christine Ertel and Verena Gassner; Schlögen led by Lothar Eckhart; Hirschleitenbach watch-tower led by Christine Schwansar; Enns where Lothar Eckhart, Christine Ertel, Verena Gassner

Figure 56. The Roman tower at Tulln

Figure 57. Visiting the site of Zeiselmauer

and Claudia Luxon were the guides; Wallsee where Herma Stiglitz was the guide, the *burgus* at Bacharnsdorf directed by Hannsjörg Ubl; Mautern introduced by Herma Stiglitz (Figure 55), Barbara Draxler and Sonja Jilek; Traismauer conducted by Hannsjörg Ubl and Johann Offenberger; the topography of Zwentendorf; Tulln (Figure 56) and Zeiselmauer (Figure 57) led by Hannsjörg Ubl and Bettina Wühr; and Klosterneuburg where again Hannsjörg Ubl (Figure 58) undertook the guiding. At Linz there was a special exhibition and the group visited the Heidentor just outside Carnuntum (Figure 40).

The post-Congress excursion travelled northwards into western Slovakia and south Moravia, visiting sites in and around Bratislava (Figure 59): Rusovce (*Gerulata*), Iža (*Celamantia*), Nitra, Trenčín to see the famous inscription, the settlement at Mušov and Devín Castle.

The proceedings included 87 papers in three languages, published in two volumes.

Figure 58. Guiding by Hannsjörg Ubl

Figure 59. A grubenhaus at Bratislava-Dúbravka, Slovakia

The Fourteenth Congress, Carnuntum, Austria 1986

Publications

Vetters, H. and Kandler, M. (eds) 1990. *Akten des 14. Internationalen Limeskongresses 1986 in Carnuntum*. Wien: Der römische Limes in Österreich 30.

Kandler, M. and Vetters, H. (eds) 1986. *Der römische Limes in Österreich. Ein Führer*. Wien: Österreichische Akademie der Wissenschaften.

Reminiscences

C. Sebastian Sommer‡ (Germany)

There are a number of special memories of that Congress which I cherish. First, the wonderful wine and great company we had on the side of the Congress in any of the several 'Buschenschenken' (places where vintners serve temporarily their own wine of the last year) scattered in and around Bad Deutsch-Altenburg, the little spa-town occupying the easternmost part of Carnuntum. Second and connected with that, Willem Willems who shouted out loudly after I had introduced myself: "Ah, Sebastian 'military vici' Sommer". Third, walks to the banks of the river Danube with different colleagues enabling very interesting talks on various subjects, not all on archaeology. Fourth, the particular sulfuric smell from the healing waters of the spa accompanying the whole Congress. Fifth, the main hall of the Congress, where we gathered on top of a covered earlier swimming pool and where we had one evening 'Congress dances' and some exercises with 'Laurentia, liebe Laurentia mein …' (google it, great fun). Sixth, of the sessions held in the other section in a converted restaurant hall the thematic one initiated by David Breeze on the question of the interaction between Romans and natives at the time of the Roman conquest in the various provinces and Siegmar von Schnurbein's almost furious reaction to my suggestion that in Raetia north of the Alps no indigenous population can be found (in southern Germany we are still 'fighting' over that issue). And last, but I am not sure about this, it was during the long bus rides on the excursions of the Congress that the lasting tradition of the 'singing-bus' was established.

Bill Hanson (UK)

The Congress in Carnuntum, my third, was particularly memorable for a number of reasons. Firstly, I almost did not make it. Because I was in the middle of a major, long-running excavation (Elginhaugh), I left the acquisition of a Czechoslovakian visa (necessary for the post-Congress tour) until the very last minute. The plan was to acquire it from the embassy in London en route to the airport, but, much to my embarrassment, I discovered when I got there that my passport had just expired! I dashed to Petty France, then home of the Passport Office, to get a new one (still possible to do on the day back then) and managed to persuade someone to let me jump the queue, before grabbing a taxi back to the Czechoslovakian embassy and then on to Heathrow. I was bundled onto the flight just as they were closing the doors and realised as I sat down that I was in the First Class section. Colleagues on the same flight thought I had missed it until we were reunited on disembarkation – with me feeling all the better for the large gin and tonic imbibed en route courtesy of British Airways.

For me the field trips have always been the highlights of the Congress, providing the opportunity not only to see, but to be guided around sites that might otherwise be difficult to reach. In this case the post-Congress tour beyond the Danube certainly did not disappoint. The visit to the famous late second-century rock-cut victory inscription in Trenčín over 100 km north-west of the Danube, and to the bath-house/villa *in barbaricum* at Dúbravka, not long excavated at the time, have stayed in the memory banks. The hospitality in Czechoslovakia, still then behind the Iron Curtain, was impressive. Indeed, we were feted, fed and entertained so generously at Iža that we were very late reaching our hotel, where we were still obliged to eat the meal that had been booked for us before they would issue our room keys! There had been much singing en route and, indeed, on some of the longer journeys earlier in the Congress – the first manifestation of what later came to be more formalised as the 'singing bus' in which it has always been my great pleasure to play my part.

Siegmar von Schnurbein (Germany)

This Congress was particularly memorable for me because it was marked by numerous conversations with colleagues from the former Eastern Bloc.

First of all, there was Sigrid Dušek from Weimar, who travelled to a Limes Congress for the first time and was able to report on her sensational excavations in the Germanic pottery centre of Haarhausen. There, pottery was made entirely according to Roman techniques on a large scale, a completely new indication of the technological influence of Roman culture reaching beyond the *limes*. Since 1964, no one from the German Democratic Republic had been allowed to travel to a Limes Congress; their participation was a joyfully welcomed event, especially for those of us from the Federal Republic of Germany!

Carnuntum, with its beautiful walks along the Danube, offered us many opportunities to talk in pairs: this was most welcome, as various colleagues from the Eastern Bloc had the urgent need to be able to talk in confidence, unobserved! The resulting personal contacts made many an invitation to the Römisch-Germanische Kommission (RGK) possible in the years that followed until the fall of communism in 1990, especially thanks to the information about people who were not allowed to travel to Carnuntum.

It was depressing for all of us that Mordechai Gichon was denied the opportunity to participate in the impressive excursion to Slovakia. He, as a citizen of the State of Israel, was denied a visit visa by Czechoslovakia. With forceful words he tried to persuade the assembled colleagues to make an official protest on the part of the Congress! Hermann Vetters, as President of the Congress, found himself in a difficult situation as a result, but was unable to do anything against the 'high politics'. In the following days in Slovakia, I admired how, after the impressive visits to the various places and the wonderful invitations there, he evoked the pure peacefulness of our cross-border research and the necessity of free cooperation in the speeches of thanks. That was true diplomacy!

The Fifteenth Congress, Canterbury, England, UK 1989

The Congress took place in Canterbury in Britannia from Saturday 2 to Sunday 10 September 1989. It was preceded by the Pilgrimage of Hadrian's Wall held from Saturday 26 to Sunday 1 September.

The Congress was attended by 190 scholars from Europe, the Americas and Middle East. Dr Robert Runcie, Archbishop of Canterbury, was the patron of the Congress and its organising committee was chaired by Sheppard Frere. Other members of the committee were Tom Blagg, Hugh Chapman, Nick Fuentes, Stephen Johnson, Valerie Maxfield and Richard Reece. The Congress was based at the University of Kent at Canterbury (Figure 60).

A total of 102 papers were presented. These included overviews of recent work in Britain (David Breeze), Upper Germany and Raetia (Dietwulf Baatz), the Pannonian

Figure 60. Vivien Swan leads the singing at Canterbury in 1989, with Tilmann Bechert at the piano with, left to right, Brian Dobson, David Breeze and Jeff Davies

Figure 61. The Roman lighthouse in Dover

provinces (Jenő Fitz), North Africa (Maurice Euzennat), and the British and Continental Saxon Shores (Stephen Johnson and Raymond Brulet). In addition to the three geographically arranged sessions there were three thematic sessions: Roman and native in the frontier areas (organiser Tom Bloemers), the realities of life on the frontier (organiser Lawrence Keppie), and the problems peculiar to desert frontiers (organiser Tom Parker). A successful innovation was the presentation of poster displays: 24 posters added to and complemented material given in the lecture programme.

The excursions took place over three and a half days. These were to Canterbury, Dover Castle (notable for its Roman lighthouse, Figure 61) and the Painted House, the Saxon Shore forts at Richborough, Lympne, Portchester Castle (Figure 62) (where

Figure 62. The late Roman fort at Portchester Castle

Figure 63. The Ermine Street Guard on parade

Figure 64. Tom Parker gets instructions on *ballistae* from the Ermine Street Guard with Sonja Jilek, right

the Ermine Street Guard performed a display – Figures 63 and 64) and Pevensey Castle, and London. Here there was a tour of the Roman walls led by John Maloney, an exhibition of Roman military equipment and the inspection of an excavation. There was also a visit to the British Museum, where the Congress was welcomed by the director Sir David Wilson to an after-hours visit and reception. There were several other receptions: by English Heritage at Dover Castle; the Museum of London; Dover District Council; Canterbury City Museum; while there was an organ recital in Canterbury Cathedral. Guiding was in English, French (Marcis Okun) and German (Peter Guest, Figure 65).

100 papers were published in three languages: all but 15 from the Congress, a couple of papers by scholars unable to attend plus reports on some of the poster displays first held at a Congress.

Publications

Maxfield, V.A. and Dobson, M.J. (eds) 1991. *Roman Frontier Studies 1989. Proceedings of the XVth International Congress of Roman Frontier Studies.* Exeter: University of Exeter Press.

Figure 65. Peter Guest guiding; Marten de Weerd looking on

Maxfield, V.A. (ed.) 1989. *The Saxon Shore. A Handbook*. Exeter: Exeter Studies in History 25.

Elton, H. 1992. 'Review of Roman Frontier Studies 1989 ...', in *Britannia* 23: 369-70.

Reminiscence

Carol van Driel-Murray (The Netherlands)

Canterbury sticks in my mind for the electrifying performance of David Woolliscroft, brilliantly compressing his innovative research into the few minutes left to him following some endlessly waffling top dog. It was also the scene of a dreadful attack by an elderly professor on a younger colleague, something I will never forget and for many of us encapsulated what was wrong with the old days.

The Sixteenth Congress, Rolduc Abbey, Kerkrade, the Netherlands 1995

The Congress took place at the Abbey of Rolduc, Kerkrade, in the Netherlands in the Roman province of Gallia Belgica from Friday 25 to Thursday 31 August 1995. The pre-Congress tour was to North-West Germany from Tuesday 22 to Friday 25 August and the post-Congress tour from Friday 1 to Saturday 2 September to late Roman sites in Gallia Belgica.

There was a long gap between Congresses due to the earlier decision to go to the (former) Yugoslavia in 1992 but political circumstances there prevented that. Colleagues in the Netherlands and Belgium stepped forward and undertook the organisation of a Congress in the Low Countries, later than anticipated owing to the necessity to avoid a clash with the meeting of the *Fautores* (Roman pottery congress) as well as the time required to organise an unexpected Congress.

The Congress organising committee included colleagues from the Netherlands, Belgium, Germany and the UK chaired by Willy Groenman-van Waateringe. Over 200 people attended the Congress from 18 countries in Europe, America, Africa and the Near East (Figure 66). Ninety-two lectures were held over four days in three parallel

Figure 66. The participants of the Congress at Rolduc, 1995

Figure 67. The pre-Congress excursion in 1995 included a visit to Kalkriese

sessions. Three days were devoted to themes and this arrangement was reflected in the organisation of the proceedings of the Congress. The themes were: the geography of Roman frontiers; problems of river frontiers versus artificial frontiers; problems of late defence; across the frontier; problems of the relationship between buildings in forts and extra-mural settlements; resources and supply. However, there was a substantial collection (about half the lectures) of 'Miscellanea'. A special evening lecture was given by Michel Reddé and Siegmar von Schnurbein on their recent excavations at Alésia.

During the Congress, delegates visited the Rhine *limes* in the Netherlands. One day was spent in Nijmegen, where five lectures were delivered on the military and civilian sites followed by visits to excavations and the G. M. Kam Museum where there was an exhibition on 'Cavalry from the Low Countries in the Roman army'. The tour along the frontier included Vechten (*Fectio*) where the Congress was greeted by A. Nuis, the State Secretary for Education, Culture and Science, and also to Alphen aan den Rijn and Zwammerdam. At Leiden, the Congress was welcomed by the Director of the Rijksmuseum and inspected a special exhibition on Roman Valkenburg. The Congress also visited the Thermenmuseum in Heerlen and the Bonnefanten Museum in Maastricht.

At the end of the Congress the thanks of the delegates to the city of Kerkrade was given by Denis Saddington in Afrikaans, Latin and English (quoting Tennyson, Cowper and Elgar), each delivered to the enthusiastic reception of his audience.

The pre-Congress excursion explored early military activities in Germania including Anreppen, Haltern and Kalkriese (Figure 67), the suspected site of the Battle of the Teutoburg Forest. Moving to the other chronological end of the Empire, the focus of the post-Congress excursion lay with late Roman military installations in Belgium and France (Figures 68, 69 and 70).

The proceedings of the Congress included 89 papers in three languages.

Publications

Groenman-van Waateringe, W., van Beek, B.L., Willems, W.J.H. and Wynia, S.L. (eds) 1997. *Roman Frontier Studies 1995. Proceedings of the XVIth International Congress of Roman Frontier Studies. Roman Frontier Studies.* Oxford: Oxbow Monograph 91.

Bechert, T. and Willems, W.J.H. 1995. *Die Römische Reichsgrenze zwischen Mosel und Nordseeküste.* Stuttgart: Theiss.

Fiema, Z.T. 1999. 'Review of Roman Frontier Studies 1995 …', in *American Journal of Archaeology* 103 (2): 348.

Figure 68. The post-Congress tour in 1995 explored sites and excavations in Belgium

Figure 69. Tongeren in 1995. From left: Gerry Friel; Pete Wilson; Jacqueline Hoevenberg and Tony Wilmott with Mordechai Gichon entering.

Figure 70. The forum at Bavay

The Sixteenth Congress, Rolduc Abbey, Kerkrade, The Netherlands 1995

Reminiscences

Maureen Carroll (UK)

My first Limes Congress was in 1995 in Rolduc. I was working in Cologne for the Archäologische Bodendenkmalpflege, based in the Römisch-Germanisches Museum, and I gave a paper on my work on the late Roman fort of Deutz-Divitia on the Rhine. The conference was such a great experience for me, largely because of the very upbeat, friendly, and supportive colleagues I met. The international nature of the conference, with colleagues from Britain, the Netherlands, Belgium, Romania, Germany, and from the other side of the Atlantic (like me, originally!), was exhilarating. People who stick out in my mind are David Breeze, Bill Hanson, Raymond Brulet, Vivien Swan, and many others. It seemed to me to be a conference as a conference should be, with days of lectures and whole days of excursions to get to know each other and the sites better. My lasting memory of presenting on Deutz-Divitia was how positive the response was (apart from Bill Hanson pointing out how I had got hectares and acres all wrong—I am an idiot when it comes to numbers). It is a bit of a German national academic sport to pick apart and criticise a speaker at a conference or a seminar, and I had just been through that at a recent workshop in Frankfurt where I reported on Deutz. Basically the same paper in two different circumstances received such a different response. It made me put things in a healthy perspective and I appreciated the support from colleagues whose views and knowledge I respected! And I knew that I would be coming to this conference in future, as long as I had something to say, and to meet up again with colleagues who had become friends.

Harry van Enckevort (The Netherlands)

This was my first Limes Congress. From the first day of the pre-Congress excursion, starting in Osnabrück on 22 August 1995, to the last day of the post-Congress excursion in Bavay on 2 September, it was a waterfall of impressions. Most of the participants slept in the Rolduc Abbey's guest quarters, which was special. After dinner, some went for a walk in the vicinity before going to sleep, but a regular group descended the stairs to the basement of the abbey every evening, looking for the door of the Verloren Zoon (Lost Son, Luke 15:11). Under the brick arched roof of this underground bar, existing friendships were confirmed and new ones made, while the necessary alcoholic refreshments were consumed. Very special. I think back to it during each subsequent Congress.

On the first excursion day in Nijmegen, I gave a lecture in the morning on 'Die Belegung des frührömischen Lagers auf dem Kops Plateau'. In the afternoon, I explained the excavations on the plateau to the participants. A year later, the proceedings of the Congress were published and it turned out that the word 'Belegung' in the title of my contribution had been changed into 'Belegerung' by one of the editors, so that title and text no longer matched! The second day of excursions went to the west of the Netherlands. Impressive was the meeting there in a large marquee on the terrain of the excavation in Vechten, next to the motorway. In his characteristic way, David Breeze gave a speech on behalf of the Congress about the importance of Roman archaeology in the Netherlands to the Dutch State Secretary Ad Nuis. In it, concerns were expressed about the poor protection of the most important Roman sites along the Dutch *limes*. It was not until 26 years later, on 27 July 2021, that UNESCO's World Heritage Committee placed these sites under the heading of 'Frontiers of the Roman Empire – The Lower German Limes' on the World Heritage List.

Tony Wilmott (UK)

The Limes Congress had always been a mythical occasion to me, since the late Charles Daniels spoke of it in lectures when I was an undergraduate at Newcastle. I remember his excitement when he returned from the 1976 Congress in Hungary. After graduation I moved away from the frontier for a decade before returning to excavate Birdoswald in 1987. My first real encounter was in 1989, when the Hadrian's Wall Pilgrimage was the pre-Congress excursion. The Pilgrims came to Birdoswald, and I had arranged to have the site looking its absolute best for this important visit. The trouble was, I had to conclude the excavation while the Limesforscher assembled in Canterbury, so I missed the Congress. In some disappointment I did my own pilgrimage to the walls in Berlin and China instead. I thought it unlikely that I would have a chance at another Limes Congress. How wrong could I be – I have attended every one since. My first was in 1995 in Rolduc (Figure 69). It was rather bewildering and a bit intimidating. There were so many people whose books I had read, and whose work I had read about, and I had to stand in front of them and talk about my work. I needn't have worried. I rapidly felt at ease, and by the end, I was among friends, and those friendships have endured. An abiding memory was that esteemed colleagues would burst into song on the bus trips. A few German colleagues came across to what was still a designated English language bus to join in. And that, I believe, was the real genesis of what became the 'Singing Bus'.

The Seventeenth Congress, Zalău, Romania 1997

The Congress took place in Zalău in the Roman province of Dacia Porolissensis in Romania between Monday 1 and Wednesday 10 September 1997. The pre-Congress tour started in Budapest on Saturday 30 August and consisted of a two-day tour through 'Barbaricum'.

The Chairman of the organising committee was Nicolae Gudea (Figure 114), supported by a committee including Alexandru Matei (Figure 71), Mircea Chişu and Stelian Potroviţă. The Congress was attended by 204 delegates from Europe, North America, Australia, Asia and Africa.

Thirteen speeches were delivered during the course of the two-hour long opening ceremony, including by the commander of the 4th army group. Over five days, 106 lectures were delivered in five sections: general reports on the provinces; excavations and research on the *limes*; the Roman army and military history; the daily life of the Roman soldier; Romans and barbarians on the frontiers of the empire, with a special focus on the north-western borders of *Dacia Porolissensis* in north-west Dacia.

Figure 71. Alexandru Matei explaining his excavation in 1997

Figure 72. Group photo of congress participants from Zalău Congress

Excursions during the Congress included numerous sites in *Dacia Porolissensis* including: the great fort at Porolissum (Figure 72); the forts at Românași, Romita and Tihău; Sesul Tâlhăresei Hill, Buciumi fort and Poic pass; Poieni where the Congress walked along the Carpathians visiting the sites of several watch-towers (Figures 73

Figure 73. Walking through the Carpathian Mountains in Romania

The Seventeenth Congress, Zalău, Romania 1997

Figure 74. Relaxing after a long walk: includes Michaela Konrad, Andreas Thiel; at the front from the left: Stefan Groh, Sebastian Girhos, Martina Meyr, Meike Sieler, Bill Hanson & Sonja Jilek

and 74), the fort at Bologna and fortlet at Ciucea. The days of lectures and visits were enlivened by many receptions and special lunches (Figures 75 and 76).

The pre-Congress tour started at Aquincum (Budapest) in Hungary and proceeded to Porolissum, some 8km from Zalău. Exhibitions were visited at Nyíregyháza, Satu Mare and Şimleu Silvaneie, and excavations at Nyíregyháza (a Sarmatian settlement), Medieşu Aurit and Şimleu Silvaneie. The post-Congress excursion was on 11 September visiting Cluj-Napoca where there was a special exhibition on 'The daily life of the Roman soldier in Dacia', the legionary base at Turda (*Potaissa*) and the remnants of the fort at Alba Iulia (*Apulum*) (Figure 77), before many boarded the night train to Vienna.

There were 86 papers in the proceedings in three languages. These were supported by several books on the Romans in Dacia produced specially for the Congress prepared by Nicolae Gudea and Siegmar von Schnurbein, and a book of abstracts of the lectures.

Publication

Gudea, N. (ed.) 1999. *Roman Frontier Studies 1997. Proceedings of the XVIIth International Congress of Roman Frontier Studies*. Zalău: County Council of Salaj.

Figure 75. The army provided lunch at Porolissum

Figure 76. Inside the tent; standing Willem Willems

The Seventeenth Congress, Zalău, Romania 1997

Figure 77. Inspecting an excavation at Alba Iulia on the post-Congress excursion

Reminiscences

Maureen Carroll (UK)

My second Limes Congress was in Zalău. This one was memorable for three reasons. Firstly, the day before I was due to fly from Cologne to the conference, Princess Diana died in that horrific car crash in Paris. I thought all the Brits at the conference would be devastated (I was wrong) and might not have the latest news, given that they were there in Romania before me and on the pre-excursion with perhaps little access to the news. So I thought it was my 'job' to report on what had happened. The reaction was a bit underwhelming, but I will always remember Diana's death and the Zalău conference together. The second big thing was that I had just been offered the job in the Department of Archaeology at the University of Sheffield, and I had accepted it. But it had to remain confidential, as I had not yet resigned from my job in Cologne, and I didn't want anything or anyone to get in the way of me leaving Cologne or sabotaging the move! My British colleagues were pleased for me, and I felt that this conference was the right place to celebrate the change in career and country. Celebrate we did (the Țuică flowed....need I say more)! And, finally, it was great to visit a country I had never been to, and the first taxi drive on very dark roads, with the occasional ox-drawn cart (no lights) avoided on the way there, was a real experience. I got to see the Danube for the first time!

Martina Meyr (Germany)

Zalău was my first Limes Congress (Figure 74). At that time I was still a student without a degree. Together with Andreas Schaub, Alexandra Gram and Hannes Lauber we drove in a VW Polo from Augsburg to Budapest where the pre-excursion started. In addition to visiting some excavations, I have fond memories of the first evening. Sitting at the table of David Breeze, Tony Wilmott, Pete Wilson and Bill Hanson I remember good conversation and lots of fun – but I had no idea who the colleagues were as they only introduced themselves by their first names.... The next morning was marked by the news of Lady Diana's death which the British colleagues informed us at the breakfast table.

The Congress itself had a great ease despite a very busy programme. In addition to lectures, excursions to excavations and museums, the evenings left lasting memories. The Romanian colleagues – supported by a huge number of students – made sure that we had dinner together every evening followed by a party. Unforgettable was Tom Parker, who after the proposal to hold the next Congress in Jordan was accepted (and where the voting was for either Jordan or Israel), danced to 'California Dreamin' with a bottle of orange-flavoured vodka in his hand and at '.... and I began to pray' fell onto his knees on the dance floor. This song became obligatory in the singing bus at all following Congresses and the duo with Tony Wilmott became a must-have on every excursion.

But also meetings with colleagues from different countries and various stages in their careers in the only pub on the market square were extremely enriching. Here scientific questions were discussed, lectures talked about and a few beers were drunk. You couldn't avoid each other in this small town and thus had a great group experience. There is still so much to tell.... The room I shared with Tony Wilmott; other colleagues' hotel, where water was available only a few hours per day and Paul Austin accidentally brushed his teeth with Țuică; all the schnapps in plastic coke bottles; huge packages of books; friendships that still exist since then; Sebastian Sommer, who ran after his rolling toilet paper roll in the forest near Porolissum; lunch in the military tent at Porolissum; Steve Sidebotham's lecture on Berenice – or how slides became a film; the freshly excavated gate of a fort with building inscription; women who thanked us because they now had a paved road into their village; the excursion buses, accompanied by police and ambulances, meandered through deserted areas; outhouses in backyards of town halls and mayors with sashes... What remains is a wonderful memory and a feeling that is difficult to describe – I cannot decide whether it was because it was my First Congress or because this one in Zalău was very special.

The Eighteenth Congress, Amman, Jordan 2000

The Congress was held in Amman in Jordan in the Roman province of Arabia from Saturday 2 to Monday 11 September 2000.

This was the first time in over 50 years and 17 previous occasions that the Congress had visited an Arab country and only the second time a meeting had been held outside Europe. The Chair of the Congress committee was David Breeze, working with Phil Freeman from the University of Liverpool, which undertook the administration for the Congress, with support from the Council for British Research in the Levant, in particular the Director Alison McQuitty and her successor Bill Finlayson. The Patron of the Congress was H.R.H. Prince Hassan bin Talal (Figure 78) who took a keen interest in the Congress, together with his daughter H.R.H. Princess Sumaya bint Hassan, and invited the entire Congress to a formal dinner on 6 September. Support

Figure 78. HRH Prince Hassan arrives to welcome the Congress to Jordan. From left, Mrs Sindall, Mr Sindall, Chair of the Council for British Research in the Levant, David Breeze, Siegmar von Schnurbein, HRH Prince Hassan, HRH Princess Sumaya

Figure 79. The Congress in Jordan

Figure 80. Siegmar von Schnurbein addresses the Congress

also came from the Jordanian Department of Antiquities, Director Ghazi Bisheh and his successor Fawwaz al Khraysheh, and the Minister of Tourism, H.E. Akel Biltaji.

The Congress was attended by 250 participants from 25 countries (Figure 79). Over 150 lectures were delivered, starting with five on Roman archaeology in Jordan. The remainder were largely organised geographically though with special sessions on the Roman army, Roman fortifications, documents and archives, and, a new initiative, fleets and frontiers (Figure 80).

Five coaches, each with a guide and support, themselves a very eclectic group, transported the Congress round the Roman sites. Half-day visits were undertaken to Roman Amman led by Ignacio Arce of the Spanish Archaeological Mission Jordan, and Jerash hosted by the Department of Antiquities of Jordan. The first expedition was to North Jordan visiting the fort at Qasr al-Azraq (Figure 81), the small fort at Qasr Huwwinit, the forts at Dier al-Kahf and Umm el-Quttein, the Nabataean, Roman and Byzantine town at Umm el-Jimal, and the *via nova Traiana*. The second tour was of Central Jordan embracing the forts at Qasr Bshir, Khirbet el-Fityan and el-Lejjun, and the Nabataean temple at Al-Qasr (Figures 82 and 83). The final excursion, to South Jordan, ran over two days on 10 and 11 September visiting the Roman forts at Da'janiya and Udhruh with the culmination of the Congress being a day at Petra. The tours in the heat of the desert had led to the appearance of several exotic headdresses and as a result a prize was offered for the best headdress; it was awarded to Alexandra

Figure 81. Colin Wells walks away from Qasr el-Azraq, originally a Roman fort, much changed in later centuries and the desert headquarters of T.E. Lawrence (of Arabia) in the First World War

Figure 82. Crossing the desert to visit Qasr Bshir

Figure 83. Tom Parker greets the Congress; behind him in blue shirt and green hat Hans Ulrich Nuber; far right is Ioana Bogdan Cătăniciu.

Gram, with Vivien Swan in second place. Subsequent prizes have been offered for the best poster and the best lecture by participants under the age of 35.

Members of the Congress were welcomed by many institutions in Jordan. A reception was hosted by the British Embassy and the Council for British Research in the Levant in the grounds of the Ambassador's Residence (Figures 84, 85 and 86). The Department of Antiquities provided a lavish feast during the visit to Jerash. At the American Center of Oriental Research the Director, Pierre Bikai and his wife Patricia, hosted a reception and introduced the Congress to the work of the Center. After the closing session the Darat Al Funun – Abdul Hameed Shoman Foundation hosted a reception and tour of its premises on Jebel Amman. On the arrival of the Congress at Petra, the Petra Regional Council hosted a reception and dinner.

Delegates were able to organise additional tours with several arriving early or staying on to take advantage of travelling around Jordan, Syria and Israel. Two delegates opted to take their time on the outward journey, walking from London to Amman. David Kennedy, author of the handbook which accompanied the Congress (Figure 87), together with Bob Bewley, organised a flight over Amman and Jerash for around 20 delegates in an antiquated Soviet-era helicopter (Figure 88).

The publication of the proceedings was coordinated by the University of Liverpool with 100 papers (of the 150+ given at the Congress) published in three languages.

Figure 84. Gabriele Rasbach, Andreas Thiel, Kirsten Thiel and Franz B. Maier, with Willem Willems in the background at the British Ambassador's reception.

Figure 85. Rebecca Jones, Fraser Hunter, Carol Davies and Jeff Davies at the British Ambassador's reception

Figure 86. Mark Steel, Walter and Helen Cockle and Roberta Tomlin at the British Ambassador's reception

Figure 87. David Kennedy, who wrote the handbook for the Congress, centre, with David Breeze and Zsolt Visy

Figure 88. Delegates boarding the helicopter for a flight over Amman and Jerash

Publications

Freeman, P., Bennett, J., Fiema, Z.T. and Hoffmann, B. (eds) 2002. *Limes XVIII. Proceedings of the XVIIIth International Congress of Roman Frontier Studies held in Amman, Jordan (September 2000).* (British Archaeological Reports International Series 1984). Oxford: Archaeopress.

Kennedy, D. 2000. *The Roman Army in Jordan.* London: Council for British Research in the Levant.

James, S. 2005. 'Limesfreunde in Philadelphia: a snapshot of the State of Roman Frontier Studies', *Britannia* 36: 499-502.

Reminiscences

Rebecca Jones (UK)

Working in Scotland, I had heard so much from David Breeze and Bill Hanson about the Congress in Romania that I realised that I really needed to attend one, thinking that I would be able to in 1999 when it returned to Britain (which of course, it didn't). But I was fortunate to be able to attend the Congress in Amman instead, having recently completed a year as a researcher on Roman Wales with Jeff Davies at the University of Aberystwyth.

The Congress did not disappoint. In many ways, attending your First Congress can be overwhelming – all the great and the good of Roman frontier archaeology attend, but the trips were a great leveller. I remember us all decanting from the buses and standing in the back of cattle trucks to visit sites in the desert. If you weren't on the first truck, then you found yourself caked in sand from the trucks in front of you (Figure 82). I remember gazing in awe at Qasr Bshir, Tony Wilmott and I marvelling at the inscription at the entrance and wondering why we scrabbled around on the northern frontiers of Britain. I remember marvellous buffets and feasts, sadly marred by a slight bout of food poisoning the evening we were all taken out for a formal dinner by Prince Hassan (I gave my paper the following day, clutching onto the lectern). On the final overnight trip down to Petra there had been errors in the room bookings but David Breeze and Sonja Jilek re-arranged everyone so that we all had a bed! That post-Congress trip was my first experience of the 'singing bus', and many of the songs invented at that Congress are now regularly sung at Congresses (the 'Via Nova Traiana' and 'It's a long way to Da'janiya' spring to mind)!

Martina Meyr (Germany)

There are an incredible number of things to tell about the Limes Congress in Amman. So I will limit myself to a few impressions. It started at the opening session where all of us were invited to a reception at the British Embassy that evening and a Jordanian princess was also introduced. Well, the beautiful princess, despite having bodyguards, had the full attention of a lot of colleagues! The others managed to empty the embassy's entire alcoholic supplies (beer, wine, whisky and gin). For sure the ambassador didn't expect that when he extended the invitation.

Even more impressive was the dinner with the then Crown Prince Hassan bin Talal and his wife Princess Sarvath al-Hassan in the basement of a posh hotel. A multi-course menu was served at tables with white tablecloths and chair covers – without alcohol, of course. In the end everyone was allowed – or rather had to – say goodbye to the crown prince couple. Since very few wore appropriate clothing, the lack of knowledge of courtly manners was probably excused. And then there were excursions

Figure 89. Martina Meyr in the desert

on cattle trucks, the almost completely preserved Qasr Bshir fort in the middle of the desert, the song 'There is no beer in Lejjun' was born, white sofas in one of the conference rooms, hummus and foul, entering Petra like Indiana Jones (well, not all of us on a horse) and the Red Sea.....(Figure 89).

The Nineteenth Congress, Pécs, Hungary 2003

The Congress took place in Pécs in Hungary in Pannonia Inferior from Sunday 1 to Sunday 8 September 2003. The Congress was preceded by a meeting of the Roman Military Equipment Conference in Vienna from Wednesday 27 to Friday 29 August, the pre-Congress taking the form of the journey to Pécs along the Danube. The post-Congress tour ventured into the Great Hungarian Plain.

The Congress was organised by the Department of Ancient History and Archaeology at the University of Pécs under the leadership of Zsolt Visy (Figure 90) and held under the Patronage of Dr Ferenc Mádl, President of the Republic of Hungary. Almost 240

Figure 90. Zsolt Visy gets the Congress delegates ready for a group photograph

Figure 91. Participants discuss applying for European funding for the Frontiers of the Roman Empire project in a wine cellar at Ilok, Croatia. From left: Ángel Morillo; Michel Reddé; Sonja Jilek; David Breeze; Andreas Thiel; Egon Schallmayer; Sebastian Sommer; Ján Rajtár; Rebecca Jones; Zsolt Visy; Siegmar von Schnurbein; Mirjana Sanader and Mihail Zahariade.

scholars from 27 countries attended the Congress with almost 150 lectures and 20 poster presentations. The focus of the presentations was by theme: epigraphy and history; how did frontiers actually work?; Roman frontiers and barbarians; civilians on frontiers; the material culture of the supply, preparation and consumption of food and drink; soldiers and religion; military architecture and material culture, with the remaining lectures grouped chronologically rather than by province.

During the Congress, delegates visited military installations in southern Hungary. The first day took the Congress to Szekszárd with its collection of altars, the fort at Dunaszekcső from where the fortified river post could be seen on the opposite bank, and the Wosinsky Mór Museum. The tour proceeded into Croatia to visit some of the sites and sculpture at Osijek and Ilok. An evening visit to a wine cellar in Ilok provided the opportunity for the meeting of various Roman frontier managers to discuss the potential for collaborating and applying for European Union funding for joint activities (Figure 91). A second day included the museum at Paks, the fort at *Lussonium* (Dunakömlőd), the late Roman fortlet at Paks-Dunakömlőd, and the Roman altars at Bölcske where there was a display of folk dancing by local school children (Figure 92). The main visit that day was to Dunaújváros (*Intercisa*). Here the exhibition, originally laid out by Zsolt Visy, was inspected, followed by a walk through the fort, the extra-

Figure 92. Local school children perform a dance for the delegates

mural settlement, and the museum. *Gorsium* was visited on the return journey. The final excursion was to Budapest, visiting Nagytétény Roman fort (*Campona*) en route. The archaeological park and other remains in *Aquincum* were admired as well as the displays in the Hungarian National Museum in Budapest. Pécs itself was not neglected with a tour and discussion of the management of the early Christian necropolis as a World Heritage Property. Delegates were impressed by the volume and quality of stone inscriptions and sculpture on display in the various *lapidaria* visited.

The day before one excursion it rained heavily. So it was decided that the delegates could not undertake the proposed excursion the next day owing to the dangerous ground conditions. The excursion and lectures for the next two days were reversed. It was only as the Congress progressed that it was realised what was involved, not only the coaches, venues and mayors, but food and drink, crockery and cutlery, tables and tablecloths ... and portaloos.

The Congress was preceded by the 14th Roman Military Equipment Conference (RoMEC) in Vienna on the subject of 'Destructions' organised by Sonja Jilek. The pre-Congress tour took the form of the journey from Vienna to Pécs visiting sites in Austria, Slovakia and Hungary including Devín Castle, the fort at Bratislava (*Gerulata*) (Figure 93), exhibitions of Roman carved stones and museums in Mosonmagyaróvár, the fort at *Quadrata*, the *lapidarium* at Komárno, the fort at Iža (*Celemantia*), Komárom

Figure 93. Visiting the Roman fort at *Gerulata* on the pre-Congress excursion

Museum, the Roman carved stones at Igmánd, the late fort at Tokod, Esztergom, and the open air museum at Szentendre (*Ulcisia Castra*).

The post-Congress excursion visited monuments of the Sarmatians on the Great Hungarian Plain and the Móra Ferenc Museum in Szeged, Zsolt's home town.

The handbook edited by Zsolt Visy, *The Roman Army in Pannonia*, was but one of many publications produced to time with the Congress. Special mention should be made of the 80th birthday celebrations at *Aquincum* for Klára Póczy, the doyenne of Roman archaeology in Hungary, and who had guided participants on the 1976 Congress round *Aquincum* (Figure 94). The proceedings contained 99 papers in three languages.

Publications

Visy, Zs. (ed.) 2005. *Limes XIX, Proceedings of the XIXth International Congress of Roman Frontier Studies, Pécs, Hungary, September 2003*. Pécs: University of Pécs.
Visy, Zs. (ed.) 2003. *The Roman Army in Pannonia. An Archaeological Guide of the Ripa Pannonica*. Pécs: Teleki László Foundation.
Bidwell, P. 2008. 'Review of Limes XIX ...', in *Britannia* 39: 414-5.

Figure 94. 80th birthday celebrations for Klára Póczy with a presentation from Orsolya Lang

Reminiscences

Orsolya Lang (Hungary)

The very first Limes Congress that I attended was at Pécs, thus 'home advantage'. Nevertheless, it was not only the Congress itself or the papers that impressed me but also the excursion to *Aquincum*, where I had the chance and privilege to be one of the guides on the buses and show the sites of Roman Budapest to the, at that time, mainly unknown colleagues. Arriving to the legionary fortress I took 'my group' around the conserved ruins of the southern gate, the House of the Centurion and the Greater Bath (*Thermae Maiores*) and remember the interest all showed and the questions coming from Birgitta Hoffmann, Tony Wilmott and David Breeze. The crowning moment of the whole day was the 80th birthday greeting for Klára Póczy when I had a tiny role again, saying a few words on behalf of the 'young generation of *Aquincum* archaeologists' (Figure 94). It was a truly memorable day for me!

Esperanza Martín Hernández (Spain)

Not always does one have the opportunity to go to a Congress like the Limes. That's why, when Ángel Morillo asked me to go to Pécs before starting to organise the one in León, I thought it was a splendid idea. Putting faces to all those people you've been reading about for ages is something awesome. Once I was there, I remember the indecision about which lectures to attend, due to the lack of time. Over coffee, Zsolt Visy recommended to me to flip a coin to decide which one to listen to. Pécs turned out to be a charming city and I remember with tremendous fondness the nights of laughter and beers we spent there. In just one day the 'newcomers' were already part of a big family. We got to know the Hungarian pálinka and goulash, I don't know if it should go in the chapter of successes or in the chapter of tears. The excursions they took us to, the museums and camps, were exceptional. But I remember the absolute shock of entering *Aquincum* while talking with David Breeze and Sonja Jilek, what an amazing place.

However, the memory that stayed with me most strongly was the incredible willingness of everyone offering to lend a hand for the next Congress. It didn't matter if we were in Mosonmagyaróvár, Komárno, or in the *Quadrata* or *Campona* forts … Everyone I spoke to offered their help and knowledge without hesitation. It was something that struck me, I had never felt so much 'family' at a conference before.

Ioana Oltean (Romania / UK)

I had already participated in my first Limes Congress in 1997 at Zalău as a student volunteer, helping the organisers to run the event. There, I had already met numerous colleagues who returned to Pécs in 2003. However, the latter was the first time I joined as a participant, presented my research and was delighted to have exciting discussions about it with some of the most prominent scholars present.

My memories about the 2003 Hungarian Congress are a whirlwind of great research presentations, wonderful sites and impressive museums, full of exciting material. If one can ever have too many *lapidaria* – this particular Congress came pretty close to that mark! Despite this, I finally had the opportunity to 'meet' the owner (or rather his epitaph) of the Bruckneudorf/Parndorf villa where I had already excavated for two seasons a few years before under the lead of Dr. Zabehlicky, a dedicated Limes Congress participant himself. Also, I gratefully learned to see the non-classical beauty of the *Ulcisia Castra* (Szentendre) *stelae*.

It would be hard to forget the trip in Croatia, where sadly the material evidence of the recent conflict, still visible in bullet-marked buildings and in the burning of every other house in the villages we drove through, overshadowed its fabulous *limes* heritage. Boundaries, ancient and modern were ever so present: in another first, I got my passport full with stamps! Much of this happened during the pre-Congress tour, where the constant crossing of the Danube boundary brought not only repeated exit and entry stamps for me, but also some considerable delay while my Romanian passport was singled-out for detailed checks every time a country was entered and exited, much to the amusement of my colleagues on the singing bus. The roars of laughter when Bill Hanson got his passport double-looked at, just because he was sitting next to me, are still ringing in my ears after all this time!

In 1997 at Zalău I had the good fortune to experience a very different academia than the one I was familiar with, one that I was happy to join; but it was Pécs 2003 that signalled for me the end of an era and the beginning of a new one. I left the Congress early, after a mind-blowing visit to the National History Museum in Budapest, to go to my first lectureship interview.

The Twentieth Congress, León, Spain 2006

The Congress was held in León, Spain in the Roman province of Hispania Tarraconensis from Monday 4 to Monday 11 September 2006. The pre-Congress tour started in Madrid on Friday 1 September and continued by way of Numancia to León. The post-Congress tour, from Tuesday 12 to Thursday 14 September, was to north-west Spain.

The president of honour of the Congress was His Majesty the King of Spain and the Congress was organised by the Archaeological Area of the Department of Classical Studies at the University of León, under the leadership of Ángel Morillo Cerdán, with Esperanza Martín Hernández as the secretary. 284 delegates attended the Congress from 34 different countries. Almost 200 papers were read and 30 posters displayed.

Figure 95. Tony Wilmott and other Congress delegates waving the flags at León

Themed sessions at the Congress were: the internal frontiers (very appropriate in Spain); the end of the frontiers and the barbarians within the Empire; the Spanish experience: a role model of conquest and occupation; the fortified town in the late Roman period; soldiers on the move; and the early development of frontiers. There were also regional sessions, one on the Roman army and a miscellany.

After the opening plenary lectures, a special *Los Pendones Leoneses* (Parade of the Banners) ceremony was organised especially for the Congress – this ceremony dates from medieval times and consists of 40 kg flags being carried and waving in the wind. Several delegates took the opportunity to join in (Figure 95). All excursions were supported by specially prepared multi-language guide-books. The first day of excursions included the pre-Roman and Roman hill fort of Campa Torres (Figure 96) and the archaeological complex of Gijón which consisted of the museum, baths and Veranes Roman villa. On this day, the City Council of Gijón hosted a reception. The

Figure 96. Eduard Nemeth, Ioana Bogdan Cătăniciu, Felix Marcu and Ovidiu Tentea during a visit to Campa Torres Archaeological and Nature Park

Figure 97. The spectacular landscape of the Roman mines at Las Médulas

highlight of the second day was the Roman mines of Las Médulas, a World Heritage property (Figure 97). On the last day, the city of León itself was scrutinised, with the Romans walls, gate and amphitheatre inspected.

The numbers attending the pre-Congress excursion, 140, exceeded total numbers at all the early Congresses. The excursion started with a reception (with Spanish wine, no less) at the National Archaeological Museum in Madrid. The main focus of the tour was the siege remains at Numancia (Figures 98), including the camps at Peña Redonda and Renieblas. Here the delegates were welcomed by the Count of Ripalda. During this visit the attendees were fortified by a reception hosted by the Regional Government of Castile and León in Soria. On the second day, the tour included the museums at Palencia and Saldaña where the City Council provided lunch. The final visit was to the Roman Villa La Tejada, Quintanilla de la Cueza.

The post-Congress tour took the participants into north-west Spain, staying in Santiago de Compostella. The hillfort of Viladonga and the World Heritage property of Lugo were visited on the first day. At Lugo, the city walls survive and also on display are baths, private houses and the museum. The second day included visits to the fort of Cidadela and the lighthouse at A Coruña, which subsequently became a

Figure 98. Esperanza Martín and Ángel Morillo (both right) explaining Numancia

Figure 99. Boris Rankov and Geoff Morley taking the ultimate photo looking up the Tower at A Coruña

World Heritage property and is also known as the Tower of Hercules (Figure 99). For British delegates, Coruña was the burial place of Sir John Moore of Peninsular War fame. It also transpired that in myth it was the place where the stone which became the Scottish Stone of Destiny departed Spanish shore for the next stage in its journey from Egypt to Ireland and thence to Iona. A wood carving in the Council Chamber of the city bears witness to the myth (Figure 100). The final day included the hillfort of San Cibrán de Las and the Roman fort of Baños de Bande. The tour ended with a reception offered by the Regional Government.

The proceedings contain 138 papers from the Congress in the usual three languages plus Spanish and published in three volumes.

Publications

Morillo, Á., Hanel, N. and Martín, E. (eds) 2009. *Limes XX. XX Congreso Internacional de Estudios sobre la Frontera Romana / Roman Frontier Studies.* Madrid: Anejos de *Gladius* 13.

Morillo, Á. and Aurrecoechea, J. (eds) 2003. *The Roman Army in Hispania. An Archaeological Guide.* León: University of León.

Figure 100. David Breeze at the wooden carving of Scotland's Stone of Destiny in the Council Chamber at A Coruña

Reminiscence

Matthew Symonds (UK)

A sense of fear descended two weeks before the Congress started. I was a doctoral student, and this was to be my first international conference. David Breeze had generously invited me to speak in a session on the early development of frontiers. Aware of what it could mean for my thesis if the arguments failed to convince, I drafted and redrafted my paper, mindful of the eminent authorities who would be present.

The pre-Congress tour provided my first inkling that these gatherings were not just exercises in academic anxiety. As I explored the ruins of Numancia, people kept coming over to introduce themselves. Everyone seemed so friendly. This impression was cemented after an evening reception. I watched a legendary *limes* scholar grinning as he reboarded the bus, his jacket pockets laden with bottles. Moments later, wine was being distributed. Inevitably, the very next pothole sent red wine cascading all over my white shirt, leaving me looking like an extra from a horror film and wondering if this would affect my credibility as a scholar (Figure 101). That was when the singing started.

León itself was glorious. Thanks to the organisers there were many treats in store, such as the stunning Las Médulas mines and A Coruña lighthouse, as well as seeing the inscription referring to the *Cilurnigi* people, which might explain the name of *Cilurnum* (Chesters) fort on Hadrian's Wall. Other memorable moments include

Tony Wilmott, Bill Hanson, and Vivien Swan regaling all comers with a rendition of 'we're singing in the rain' while sheltering from a downpour, and watching a friend asking for a vegetarian serving, only for the meat to be fished out before his eyes and the bowl handed back. When the day of my talk finally dawned, I was told it was 'very polished' – words that meant a lot. As did the sense of acceptance by this truly extraordinary international family.

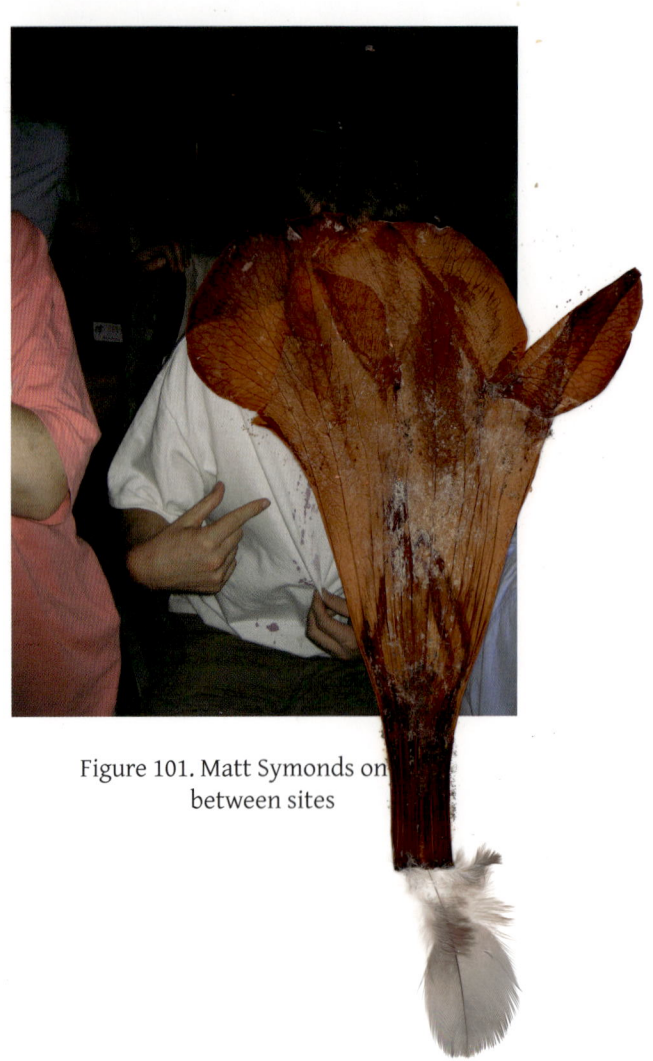

Figure 101. Matt Symonds on between sites

The Twenty-First Congress, Newcastle, England, UK 2009

The Congress was held in Newcastle upon Tyne (Britannia) from Monday 17 to Saturday 23 August 2009. The Congress was preceded by the 13th Pilgrimage of Hadrian's Wall from Saturday 8 to Friday 14 August and a pre-Congress excursion to York on Sunday 16 August.

An amazing number of 337 participants, the First Congress with more than 300 delegates, was a sign of how popular and important the Congresses have become to scholars and students alike (Figure 102).

The Congress was sponsored by Tyne and Wear Archives and Museums with Paul Bidwell and Nick Hodgson the main organisers (Figure 103 and 104). The opening ceremony was held in the Banqueting Hall of Newcastle City Centre in the presence of the Lord Mayor of Newcastle. Among the guests was Brenda Heywood (née Swinbank) who had been present at the First Congress, also held in Newcastle, 60 years earlier.

The themes for the lectures were: Roman roads; the Roman frontier in Wales; the Eastern and North African frontiers; recognising differences in lifestyles through material culture; barbaricum; Britain; Roman frontiers in a globalised world; civil settlements; death and commemoration; Danubian and Balkan provinces; camps; logistics and supply; the Germanies and Augustan and Tiberian Germany; Spain. Four sessions ran concurrently in the lecture rooms of Newcastle University.

During the tours, about 270 members of the Congress were transported in six coaches. The first day was to the hinterland of Hadrian's Wall, visiting the forts at Binchester (Figure 105), Piercebridge (Figure 103 and 104) and Whitley Castle (Figure 106). The second tour took the Congress to Yorkshire to see the fort and museum at Malton, the late Roman coastal 'signal station' at Scarborough Castle and the Roman camps at Cawthorn. A parallel tour visited the Roman forts at Hardknott and Ravenglass in the Lake District in Cumbria. The fort at Wallsend (*Segedunum*) was visited one evening. The final tour, north of the Wall, was to Risingham (*Habitancum*) and High Rochester (*Bremenium*), where the Roman cemetery at Petty Knowes was inspected (Figure 107), with an evening visit to South Shields (*Arbeia*) where there was an open-air reception and supper.

There were receptions hosted by Newcastle University and by Hadrian's Wall Heritage Ltd at the Great North Museum. On the last evening a final party, including a ceilidh, was held in the Great Hall of the Discovery Museum, courtesy of Tyne and Wear Archives and Museums.

Figure 102. Congress participants at the closing assembly

Figure 103. Nick Hodgson at Piercebridge

Figure 104. Paul Bidwell explaining Piercebridge (also Tony Wilmott)

Figure 105. David Petts explains Binchester

A pre-Congress excursion to York took place on Sunday 16 August. The visit to the remains under the Minster was led by Brenda Heywood. The walls and other Roman remains in the city were explored and a reception in the Hospitium at the Yorkshire Museum was hosted by York City Council.

There were two parallel post-Congress excursions: to Hadrian's Wall and to Roman Scotland. The Hadrian's Wall excursion visited Corbridge (*Coria*), Chesters (*Cilurnum*) (Figure 108) and Chesters Bridge, Carrawburgh (*Brocolitia*), Housesteads (*Vercovicium*), Vindolanda, Birdoswald (*Banna*), Tullie House Museum and Art Gallery, and various stretches of Hadrian's Wall and the Stanegate. The programme also included a visit to Bowness-on-Solway (*Maia*), but the site was not visited due to poor weather conditions after the group visited Tullie House. Sites inspected on the Roman Scotland excursion included Newstead (*Trimontium*), various locations on the Antonine Wall including Watling Lodge, Rough Castle fort, Seabegs Wood, Bar Hill, Croy Hill and Bearsden

Figure 106. Visit to Whitley Castle

Figure 107. Visiting the Roman cemetery of Petty Knowes near High Rochester. From left: Máté Szabó; Barry Burnham; Gerda von Bülow; Ioan Piso; Karl Strobel

Figure 108. Post-Congress tour at Chesters, from left: Graeme Stobbs, Eduard Nemeth, Tatiana Ivleva, Piotr Dyczek, Zsolt Visy, Nina Willburger

Figure 109. Bill Hanson explains the watch-tower of Muir O'Fauld

Roman bath-house. Ardoch fort, Inchtuthil legionary fortress and the watch-towers at Kirkhill and Muir o'Fauld on the Gask Ridge were visited on the final day in torrential rain (Figure 109).

There was a delay in publication with the proceedings containing 105 papers published in three languages in 2017.

Publications

Hodgson, N., Bidwell, P. and Schachtmann, J. (eds) 2017. *Roman Frontier Studies 2009. Proceedings of the XXI International Congress of Roman Frontier Studies* (Limes Congress) *held at Newcastle upon Tyne in August 2009.* (Archaeopress Roman Archaeology 25) Oxford: Archaeopress.

Bidwell, P. and Hodgson, N. 2009. *The Roman Army in Northern England.* Newcastle upon Tyne: The Arbeia Society.

Hodgson, N. 2009. *Roman Scotland. XXI International* Limes *(Roman Frontier Studies) Congress, Newcastle upon Tyne. A handbook to accompany the post-Congress excursion to Scotland, 24-26 August 2009.* Newcastle upon Tyne: Tyne and Wear Archives and Museums.

Mills, N. (ed.) 2013. *Presenting the Romans. Interpreting the Frontiers of the Roman Empire World Heritage Site.* Woodbridge: Boydell Press.

Reminiscences

Tatiana Ivleva (Netherlands)

My first Limes Congress was actually supposed to have been the one in León, but I missed an early bird registration deadline by a few days and could not afford to pay the full price. It was to be Newcastle then, and I was very excited to visit, as, firstly, I had never been to the UK before and, secondly, had never visited Hadrian's Wall either. It was the first time for everything, as on this trip I learned the expression 'British summer'. I arrived in Newcastle in August packed with sandals, T-shirts and summerish dresses. As a result, on my return home my luggage was not filled as one would expect with new exciting archaeology books, but rather with new clothes and shoes good for the late autumn and early winter...

I do not remember being particularly nervous or terrified about presenting for the first time at the Congress as I did not even know what to expect or even whom to fear most. My main concern was that I wouldn't be able to print out my talk, so I brought multiple copies safely stored in different parts of my luggage. The scariest moment, however, came when I arrived (in my summer dress) to the huge auditorium on the Newcastle University premises where the session was taking place. Seeing how with every minute the huge space started to be filled in with people, with more than a half of seats in the auditorium taken, it dawned on me that it is actually a big deal, this Limes Congress. The presentation went in a blur, and later I was told that I did not even hear the session chair and some participants asking me to speak a bit louder as from the nervous breakdown I was experiencing I had nearly lost my voice (and hearing apparently).

But apparently people heard what I was saying and appreciated it as a few days later I was told that Professor Ian Haynes whom I had only known from publications really wanted to have a chat with me about my presentation. What followed was me stalking him feverishly – on the excursion day I approached people with a question 'do you know in which bus he is sitting?". Eventually he and I found ourselves on the same bus, but I was so ashamed of my stalking attempt that I pretended something outside the bus window was more important to look at when he passed my seat. Little did I know that fast forward five years, Newcastle would become my home for two and half years, as I joined the University as Marie Curie Fellow, and that Ian would become my supervisor.

Nor do I remember this Congress as particularly wild and sleepless. What I do remember is the one-hour passport control queue at the Newcastle airport for those unfortunate to have a non-EU passport. Holder of Russian citizenship, I remember having identified the purpose of my visit as 'a frontier congress' and being told in an incomprehensible Geordie accent 'there are a bunch of your mates already here'. I remember Congress participants picking up berries which grew nearby the site of the Roman fort Piercebridge; Ian prior to the excursion promising that the buses will return to Newcastle on time for the dinner, a remark that led to group laughter, because apparently during the León Congress some excursions ran until very late at night. I got to see rural England for the first time during the excursions to the sites in the middle of nowhere – Whitley Castle, Cawthorn and Petty Knowes. I will never forget the impressive defensive earthworks of Whitley Castle. This is where my gym membership has finally paid off, as going up and down from one steep defensive ditch to another left many out of breath.

Oh, and I somehow avoided the 'singing bus' as I was told that people sang Christmas carols. I did not know any, and was ashamed to confess this, not realising that someone had simply tricked me. It took another two Limes Congresses and Rob Collins's steadfast persuasion before I finally joined the singing bus crew and realised that singing Christmas carols in the summer on the bus would be the least of my worries.

Frances McIntosh (UK)

Newcastle 2009, a volunteer's perspective

In September 2008 I started a research masters (MLitt) at Newcastle University, but did not move there until May 2009. In the summer of 2009 I was asked by my supervisors, Lindsay Allason-Jones and Ian Haynes, if I would like to volunteer for this conference called the Limes Congress, coming to Newcastle. Now I was not a frontier studies person at that point, I'd barely have called myself a Romanist (having steadfastly avoided the period in my undergraduate degree!), so I had no idea what the conference was, but gamely said yes. The volunteers were a mixed group of postgraduate students from Durham and Newcastle Universities. I don't remember everyone, but three of the Durham students were Darrell Rohl (choreography of the Antonine Wall), Joy Szigeti (Roman cremation burial in Britain) and James Taylor (Coptic monks in Egypt). We all got great t-shirts, which I still have today!

A highlight for me was visiting *Epiacum* fort, and running up and down the ditches, but also meeting Stuart Ainsworth. I had grown up watching Time Team, so for me this was an extremely exciting moment! We had tea breaks in a separate building, so one of our jobs was shepherding the delegates across a car park to get there, and not losing any of them. I distinctly remember quite a few deluges just as the breaks began, and a panicked hour when the power went off. How were 300+ delegates going to cope without caffeine?!

For me, it was my first real introduction into frontier studies, and an academic conference, so it was a real eye opener. Delegates from across the Empire (and beyond), papers on all manner of topics, many of which were completely new to me. It gave me the bug and I, along with Darrell, organised the Theoretical Roman Archaeology Conference (TRAC) in 2011 at Newcastle. Not quite the same scale, but the experience at Limes 2009 stood me in really good stead.

The Twenty-second Congress, Ruse, Bulgaria 2012

The Congress took place in Ruse, Bulgaria (Moesia inferior) from Thursday 6 to Tuesday 11 September 2012. The pre-Congress tour was from Monday 3 to Wednesday 5 September, and the two post-Congress excursions were from Wednesday 12 to Friday 14 September and on Saturday 15 September.

The leader of the Congress was Lyudmil Vagalinski (Figure 110). The management of the Congress itself was in the hands of a private 'entertainment' company who performed its task excellently. The meeting was held in the pleasant town of Ruse on the Danube, with delegates travelling via Sofia (where the pre-Congress excursion started) and also Bucharest in Romania, with Ruse having at that time, the only bridge over the Danube between Bulgaria and Romania (the New Europe Bridge, much further west, opened the following year).

The 204 lectures ran in three concurrent sessions. The themes under discussion were: fortifications and soldiers; veterans on the frontiers; families and dependents of soldiers; civil settlements, roads and trade; religion and burial rites; Rome and barbaricum (Figure 111); interdisciplinary researches; remote sensing on Roman frontiers; running and expanding the World Heritage property. The evenings were generally spent in the delightful restaurants in the main square of Ruse.

Figure 110. Lyudmil Vagalinski

The tours during the Congress were to military sites along the Danube (Figure 112). One journey was eastwards to the late fort at Tutrakan (*Transmarisca*) and the legionary base and museum at Silistra (*Durostorum*) with lunch provided at Medzhidy Tabiya fortress, part of the Ottoman fortification system during the Crimean War in the 19th century (Figure 113 and 114). A second was westwards to *Iatrus*, a late

Figure 111. Since the First Congress, the study of the relationship between the Roman Empire and people beyond has been constantly on the rise, with Danish scholars being one key group contributing to this growth. From left: Jonas Sigurdsson, Annette Fröhlich, Ulla Lund Hansen and Svend Erik Albrechtsen.

Figure 112. Congress participants relaxing by the Danube after a visit to the Roman fort *Dimum*

Figure 113. Florian Matei-Popescu, George Cupcea, Călin Timoc enjoying lunch at the Ottoman fortress Medzhidy Tabiya; also Raymond Brulet

Figure 114. Nicolae Gudea at Medzhidy Tabiya

Roman fort, the great legionary base at Svishtov (*Novae*), where the delegates were under the direction of Piotr Dyczek (Figure 115) and treated to displays by the *Legio I Italica* (Figure 116). The Roman remains at Belene (*Dimum*) and *Sexaginta Prista* in Ruse were also visited (Figure 117).

The pre-Congress excursion started in Sofia and concentrated on sites in the hinterland of the riverine frontier. Places visited included the late Antique and medieval site of Cherven, the delightful ruins of *Nicopolis* ad *Istrum*, Veliko Tarnovo

Figure 115. Piotr Dyczek explains the fortress at *Novae*

Figure 116. *Legio I Italica* at *Novae* (Svishtov)

Figure 117. Carol van Driel-Murray at *Sexaginta Prista*

and the medieval fortress of Tsarevets, the historical museum and the Roman road station at Storgozia in Pleven while the legionary fortress at *Oescus* on the Danube was passed on the journey to Ruse.

There were two post-Congress excursions. The first, from Wednesday 12 to Friday 14 September, visited *Abritus* and Razgrad, Madara Rider, Shumen fortress and the historical museum, Kaliakra, Balchik, Varna and its archaeological museum and Roman baths. The second was a one-day excursion on Saturday 15 September to the *Tropaeum Traiani* at Adamclisi in Romania.

The proceedings contained 119 papers in three languages.

Publications

Vagalinski, L. and Sharankov, N. (eds) 2015. *Limes XXII. Proceedings of the 22nd International Congress of Roman Frontier Studies, Ruse, Bulgaria, September 2012*. Sofia: Bulletin of the National Archaeological Institute 42.

Vagalinski, L., Sharankov, N. and Torbatov, S. (eds) 2012. *The Lower Danube Roman Limes (1st-6th C. AD)*. Sofia: National Archaeological Institute and Museum, Bulgarian Academy of Sciences.

Collins, R., Symonds, M. and Weber, M. (eds) 2015. *Roman Military Architecture on the Frontiers. Armies and their Architecture in Late Antiquity*. Oxford: Oxbow.

Figure 118. Martin Lemke and Sebastian Sommer by the banks of the Danube at Ruse

Reminiscences

Martin Lemke (Poland)

By 2012, I had been a member of the team excavating at *Novae* for a decade and also participated in the FRE Culture 2000 project from 2005-2008. I had also just finished my PhD on the *limes* in Moesia inferior, which is relevant insofar as there was a whole number of people I 'knew' quite well from their publications without having ever met them in person. So the Congress would be a premiere for me in meeting the '*limes* society' (apart from the small group I got to know during the FRE project). In particular, I remember being somewhat starstruck when being kindly introduced by Beccy Jones to Boris Rankov, whose works I had thoroughly studied for my dissertation but, more importantly, whom I admired for having a rule in sports (rowing) named after him ('Rankov-rule'). I was able to ask him a few questions on both aspects of his career over a beer in one of the outdoor pubs on Svoboda Square in Ruse.

I also remember the responsibility of co-hosting a session with Beccy and the difficulty of containing myself so as to not get carried away during a verbal altercation with one of the elders of the *limes* community after my own presentation. Speaking of responsibilities, it was both that but also a pleasure to be part of the team showing the participants around *Novae*, when the excursion reached the legionary fortress on the Danube.

Overall, the scholarly, professional (occasionally heated) atmosphere of the Congress sessions was very interesting but hardly unexpected. What surprised me more was the significant air of comradery and common purpose within such a large and very diverse group, something that could be noticed in the dynamic of the 'general assembly' on the first and last day, in separate parts of the collective (e.g. the infamous 'singing buses') and lastly in spontaneous small subgroups like the one which included among others the aforementioned Beccy Jones, the late Sebastian Sommer and myself, going for a very relaxed but still educational small stroll to the ruins of *Sexaginta Prista* in Ruse on one of the last days of the conference (Figure 118).

Simon Sulk (Germany)

My First Congress was in Ruse. The German Limes Commission prepared the proposal to host the following one in Ingolstadt in 2015. I was asked by Sebastian Sommer to join the group of German attendees to learn some organisational tricks and, more importantly, to feel the Congress spirit (or...spirit(s), which always play a big role among the *Limesfreunde*, something that I learned very quickly).

The trip to Bulgaria was quite adventurous. After the flight from Frankfurt to Budapest we met many other German archaeologists. After a three-hours-ride with a pre-booked coach, which we were not able to find at once, we finally arrived at Ruse.

I remember good and cheap hotel, food, and drinks. There were lots of excellent lectures to attend and countless new friends to make. During the excursions, we were able to see stunning places, had wonderful folkloristic receptions and were always greeted by very friendly hosts.

Right from the beginning, I felt that unique Limes Congress communal spirit which included everyone – young students and famous scholars, archaeologists from the whole Europe and beyond. I was very happy that I had the opportunity to visit Bulgaria and the Congress. Three years later, I was part of the organisation of the Ingolstadt Congress. It was an honour to welcome almost 400 delegates to Bavaria and to make sure that everyone would feel the same warmth and friendliness that I did three years earlier. Especially for those for whom Ingolstadt was their First Congress.

At last, I would like to talk about the singing bus. In 2012, I was warned not to join this 'special' company. Three years later, I voluntarily guided the singing bus with the venerable Tom Parker, Sebastian Sommer, Thomas Fischer, Bill Hanson and many more during the excursions. What else can I say other than that this is one of the best memories I will ever have of the Congress. For those who are no longer among us: we will remember.

Dmitry Karelin (Russia)

The International Limes Congress Ruse in 2012 was the first conference outside Russia for me. The two weeks of the Congress showed me quite unusual aspects of a scientific meeting with a balanced proportion of science, social, friendly communications and fun. I could even say that the last component prevailed over the others. I remember the very warm and friendly atmosphere of those days. At the very beginning it was quite difficult for me to feel really comfortable in this international academic community because in Russia there is another scientific relationship pattern, especially in communications with highly-ranked colleagues. I wanted to be introduced to several colleagues, whom I knew only by their famous books. One of them was Tom Parker. I took part in the pre-Congress excursion. When my wife and I were in the coach and the organisers started to check everybody's names I heard from the seat behind us 'my name is Tom Parker'. I realised that the person which I strongly wanted to meet and to ask so many questions about Lejjun fortress was just behind me. During the next hour of our trip I sat thinking about how to start the conversation with the famous scholar but all the plans were ruined just at the moment on the first stop on our way. We left the bus, and the next minute Tom Parker came to us and said 'Hello, I am Tom Parker. Nice to meet you...'. We spent some time chatting about our scientific and personal interests and I felt that I had met a real old friend. It was my first step into the wonderful atmosphere of the Limes Congresses. That time I wasn't familiar with many of the interesting features and traditions of this conference, I mean the singing bus, the welcoming short speeches of Congress participants at almost every place we visited, the many excursions and the possibility to see so many museums and archaeological areas, but that is another story.

The Twenty-third Congress, Ingolstadt, Germany 2015

The Congress took place in Ingolstadt in Germany (Raetia) from Monday 14 to Sunday 20 September 2015. The pre-Congress excursion started in Munich on Saturday 12 September and lasted two days. The post-Congress tour continued until Wednesday 23 September.

The principal organisers of the Congress were Sebastian Sommer (Figure 119) and Suzana Matešić with a strong supporting committee of colleagues from Bavaria and the Deutsche Limeskommission. It was the largest thus far (Figure 120), with the great number of 370 academics from 30 countries gathered at the Technical University of Ingolstadt (where once Dr Frankenstein had his laboratory). Some 210 lectures were held in four concurrent sessions, the majority in themed sessions, with about 50 posters. Numerous students from German Universities were encouraged to attend by their tutors, resulting in excellent attendance by younger scholars (Figure 121), coupled with financial sponsorship from Bavaria supporting a number of young researchers from other countries.

The themes were: recent research on the Raetian *limes*; small-scale Rome? public buildings and urban features in Roman military vici; open/closed frontiers; food and drink; waste not, want not? rubbish disposal and the Roman army; beyond the

Figure 119. Sebastian Sommer addresses the Congress

The Twenty-third Congress, Ingolstadt, Germany 2015

Figure 120. The Congress participants gathered at the fort at Eining

Figure 121. The 'Freiburger Truppe' from Freiburg University at Ingolstadt, including: Bastian Kaiser, Katharina Ramstetter, Francisco José Gómez Blanco, Szilvia Bíró, Alexandra Gram-Koch, Veronika Fischer, Lennart Schönemann, Philipp Lange, Daniel Burger-Völlmecke, Sarah Roth, Maureen Heuermann, Judith Wötzel, Sandra Schröer, Rebecca Nashan, Kathrin Lieb, Janken Kracker, Nena Sand, Prof. Dr. Alexander Heising and Lynn Stoffel

Figure 122. The miniature reconstruction at Ruffenhofen

empire's edge: visualization and strategy; signalling in the army; reconstructions of Roman fortified sites and their surroundings; presenting the Roman frontier; an imperial policy of 'defence-in-depth': a reality or a mirage; timber forts and fortresses; craftsmen, tools, techniques, machines and manufacture on the Roman *limes*; building materials; elements of construction, elements of expression; 'unpleasant to live in but it makes the city rich', industry and commerce in military and civil settlements along the *limes*; the Eastern frontier and the *limes* in North Africa; the frontier on the Danube; Roman Britain; the Rhine as a border in Lower Germany; Raetia and Upper Germany; new research on Republican and early Principate sites; Roman soldiers and religion; how to build a Roman camp; sex on the frontiers: textual and material representations of human sexuality at the edge of empire.

The large number of delegates required eight buses for the tours. On two of the days the delegates selected from a choice of tours along the Raetian *limes*. Sites on these various tours included the amphitheatre at Dambach, the archaeological park and museum at Ruffenhofen (Figure 122), the fort and bath-house at Weißenburg, the fort at Oberhochstatt, the bath-house at Theilenhofen, the burgus at Burgsalach, followed by a reception by the city of Weißenburg in the Carmelite Church. The pleasure of the

Figure 123. Boat trip on the Danube

second excursion was heightened by a boat trip along the Danube (Figure 123). The fort at Eining (Figures 120 and 124) and the legionary fortress and city of Regensburg (a World Heritage property) were the principal military places visited, with a reception hosted by the city of Regensburg in the Minoritenkirche. The final tour was to the forts at Pfünz and Böhming, the 'visualisation' of the gate at Pförring, various watch-towers and the end of the Raetian *limes*, and the *oppidum* of Manching together with its museum (Figures 125, 126 and 127).

Figure 124. Markus Gschwind introduces the fort at Eining

Figure 125. Some of the Limes ladies at the Kelten- & Römermuseum at Manching. From left: Marion Brüggler; Szilvia Bíró; Stefanie Hoss; Frances McIntosh; Beth Greene; Barbara Birley; Orsolya Lang; Carol van Driel-Murray; Sue Stallibrass; Martina Meyr; Sonja Jilek; Lara Laken; Alexandra Gram-Koch; Christiane Herb; Rebecca Jones; Tanja Romankiewicz; Snežana Golubović; Shannon Rogers Flynt; Anita Gaubatz-Sattler

Figure 126. The limes at Zandt: watch-tower 15/15: Paul Franzen, Mark Driessen, Marenne Zandstra and Carol van Driel-Murray marking the posts

Figure 127. Walking in fog to visit the *limes* at Zandt

The pre-Congress excursion took place on 12-13 September. Delegates were picked up at Munich and the tour then proceeded to its start point, the Römermuseum Boiotro in Passau. Along the frontier the fort at Künzing, the Gäubodenmuseum, St. Peter's Church and museum in Straubing and the Walhalla memorial in Donaustauf were visited.

The post-Congress excursion was to the Raetian *limes* and the Upper German *limes* in Baden-Württemberg. Sites included the archaeological park at Rainau-Buch, the 'fortlet' at Dalkingen, the fort and museum at Aalen, Schwäbisch Gmünd, the fort at Mainhardt, the *limes* at Pfahldöbel, the fort at Osterburken, ending at the Pompejanum in Aschaffenburg.

Almost 150 papers were published in two volumes and in three languages.

Publications

Sommer, C.S. and Matešić, S. (eds) 2018. *Limes XXIII. Proceedings of the 23rd International Congress of Roman Frontier Studies Ingolstadt 2015. Akten des 23. Internationalen Limeskongresses in Ingolstadt 2015.* Mainz: Beiträge zum Welterbe Limes Sonderband 4.

Matešić, S. and Sommer, C.S. (eds) 2015. *At the Edge of the Roman Empire. Tours along the* Limes *in Southern Germany.* Bad Homburg/München: Beiträge zum Welterbe Limes Sonderband 3. = *Am Rande des Römischen Reiches. Ausflüge zum Limes in Süddeutschland.*

Reminiscences

C. Sebastian Sommer‡ (Germany)

Looking back at the Congress in Ingolstadt as one of the two main organisers I have a very different perspective on it than on the other Congresses when I was a mere participant and speaker. First, there is a big gratitude towards Suzana Matešić as an extremely reliable partner in the organisation. Second, in the beginning we did not realise how many helpers were needed with so many participants – but somehow in the end enough appeared from various directions. Third, we were not happy that we were not able to show all our wonderful sites to everybody due to problems of accessibility and infrastructure in the rural areas – in the end the parallel tours turned out to have their own attraction in the sense that participants were comparing what they have seen and someone else had not. Fourth, regrettably, I remember the anger about some colleagues who had offered papers (some of them even several) but did not show up at the Congress or at least excused themselves for not being able to attend or let co-authors present the lectures – the result were quite a number of gaps in the lecture programme. And last, I remember the fun nights at the little beer halls close to the theatre after the day's worries gone, where you could be sure to meet colleagues and friends at any time of the day (and as mentioned at night, as one of the owners sold beer way after closing time, having fun with the foreigners herself).

Diana Grethlein (Germany)

The Limes Congress in Ingolstadt 2015 was the first archaeological conference I ever attended. This was during the second semester of my bachelor studies and I had – after introductions to different fields of archaeology – just decided to continue with Roman Provincial Archaeology.

I remember our professor in Freiburg, Alexander Heising, telling us students about the Congress, what a great experience taking part could be. With the Congress taking place in Germany, attendance would be easy. We applied as a group for financial assistance from the Student Council and – fortunately – got it. In the end, quite a big group of students from the Institute of Provincial Roman Archaeology at the University Freiburg in all different stages of our studies ended up attending the Congress (Figure 121).

I also remember being excited about meeting so many people, researchers whose articles and books I had read and students from other universities and especially other countries. The first days were a little overwhelming. So many interesting lectures and sessions in different rooms, always facing the decision of which session to attend. To me the whole Congress was surrounded by this special atmosphere. Everyone was included, from the young student with almost no experience in being a researcher sitting next to and talking to the long-established professor who had written several books and articles.

When I think back, I also think of the excursions, of 'Brezeln' at almost every place we visited and of very friendly people who welcomed us and who enjoyed having curious archaeologists. I've seen places and museums which left a big impression and met people who encouraged me to continue with my studies.

In the following years other, mostly smaller, conferences followed, but none could match this extraordinary experience. I later focused on Roman numismatics, changed my university and main subject but still remember this unique experience.

The Twenty-fourth Congress, Viminacium, Serbia 2018

The Congress took place in Viminacium, Serbia, after an opening day in Belgrade, both in the Roman province of Moesia Superior, from Sunday 2 to Sunday 9 September 2018.

The Congress was organised by the Institute of Archaeology in Serbia. Miomir Korać and Snežana Golubović of the Institute opened the Congress in the Hall of Heroes in the University of Belgrade (Figure 128). There followed introductory lectures by Miloje Vasić, Stefan Pop-Lazić, Nemanja Mrđić, Sofia Petković, Miroslav Vujović and Gordana Jeremić on the frontier in Serbia and its archaeology. Visits to the National Museum, Roman Belgrade (*Singidunum*) and a special exhibition on 'Roman Limes and Cities in Serbia' in the Serbian Academy of Science and Arts followed (Figure 129).

On the next day, the Congress departed for Viminacium. Here, lectures took place in a newly constructed replica Roman fort (Figures 130 and 131) and in a replica Roman villa known as the *Domus Scientiarum Viminacium*. Delegates were housed either in

Figure 128. The high table at the opening ceremony in Belgrade, from left: Andreas Thiel, Rebecca Jones, Sebastian Sommer, David Breeze, Miloje Vasić, Snežana Golubović, Miomir Korać, Stefan Pop-Lazić and Nemanja Mrđić

Viminacium or at Silver Lake and Požarevać, travelling to Viminacium daily. There were no pre- and post-Congress excursions as the delegates were able to visit the frontier in Serbia (*Pannonia* and *Moesia*) on three day-trips during the course of the Congress.

No less than 25 different themes were explored in four simultaneous sessions: mapping the edge of Empire; fortifying our frontiers; stand your ground!; *limes in fine*? Continuity and discontinuity of life in the forts of Roman frontiers; hold the line!!!; transformation of the *limes* in late Antiquity; from east to west my legions are the best; who were the *limitanei*?; first contacts between the Roman military and the local people; Rome and barbarians; small finds assemblages as a means to understanding social and economic patterns within the settlements close to Roman camps; bath buildings; building materials: elements of construction, elements of expression; a farewell to arms; production, industry and trade; life and health on the Roman *limes*; arts and crafts along the *limes*; religions and beliefs on the frontiers; Christianity at the frontiers; what about us? exploring the lives of women and children on the frontiers; Roman Egypt; the Saxon Shore; presenting the Roman frontiers; re-evaluating old excavations, are they worth it?; going wild! the roles of wild animals in life and death on the frontier.

Figure 129. Delegates catching up in Belgrade at the start of the Congress. From left: Veronica Fischer; Sophie Hüdepohl; Erik Timmermann; Ella Hetzel

Figure 130. The entrance to the replica Roman fort at Viminacium where the lectures took place

Figure 131. Boris Burandt gives a lecture

A new experiment was a debate on the purpose of Roman frontiers by eight colleagues. Each had ten minutes to make their case and then those attending the session voted. The speakers and their votes were:

    Erik Graafstal, to defend the Empire: 26
    Andreas Thiel, to control movement into and out of the province: 18
    Sebastian Sommer, to create an edge to the Empire for the Romans: 12
    Eberhard Sauer, to defend the Empire: 11
    Simon James, to keep the troops busy: 8
    Markus Gschwind, to control transhumance: 7
    Christof Flügel, to serve as a symbol and object of intimidation: 4
    Alan Rushworth, to protect travellers in the frontier zone: 1

It must be emphasised that this was a debate and all speakers acknowledged that they considered Roman frontiers were more subtle than to have but one purpose. The winner was rewarded with a mug from the Antonine Wall and a slab of chocolate depicting the Bridgeness Distance Slab from the Antonine Wall (Figure 132).

A special event was the presentation of a Festschrift to Carol van Driel-Murray and the launch of the book, *Frontiers of the Roman Empire: The Lower German Limes*, by Erik Graafstal, the late Willem Willems and Steve Bödecker, in the multi-language series of books about Roman frontiers.

Figure 132. The winner of the debate, Erik Graafstal with to his right David Breeze and Tatiana Ivleva, and to his left Anna Walas: Tatiana and Anna were in charge of counting the votes.

Figure 134. The Congress participants at the Roman fort of *Diana*

Figure 133. Visiting the Iron Gates in Serbia. From left: Orsolya Lang; Stefanie Hoss; Tatiana Ivleva; Lara Laken and Martijn Wijnhoven

Figure 135. Visiting the late Roman / Byzantine city of *Justiniana Prima*

Excursions included the Iron Gates (Figure 133), Lepenski Vir mesolithic settlement, the fort at Diana (Figure 134), the museum of the Iron Gates, Kladovo, the remains of Trajan's Bridge (the Bridge of Apollodorus), Zaječar Museum and the late Roman Palace at Gamzigrad (*Felix Romuliana*). The second excursion was to Pančevo Museum, Museum of Vojvodina in Novi Sad, and the imperial palace at *Sirmium*. The final tour took in *Justiniana Prima* (Figure 135), the museum at Leskovac, Roman villa *Mediana*, the remains of *Naissus* and the museum of Niš.

The accommodation in Viminacium was the scene of a concert as well as organised and impromptu parties: perhaps the grand 'dig hut' reminded the archaeologists of festivities on their own excavations (Figures 136 and 37).

Publications

Golubović, S (ed) 2023 Limes XXIIII. Proceedings of the 24th International Congress of Roman Frontier Studies, 2nd-9th September 2018, Viminacium - Belgrade, Serbia. Belgrade (2 volumes)

Korać, M., Golubović, S., Mrđić, N., Jeremić, G. and Pop-Lazić, S. 2014. *Rimski Limes u Srbiji/Roman Limes in Serbia*. Belgrade: Institute of Archaeology.

Korać, M., Golubović, S. and Mrđić, N. (eds) 2018. *VIVERE MILITARE EST. From Populus to Emperors - Living on the Frontier*. Belgrade: Institute of Archaeology.

Figure 136. A reception in the courtyard of the replica Roman villa – the *Domus Scientiarum Viminacium*

Figure 137. Fireworks at the end of the closing session

Reminiscence

Ivana Protić (Serbia)

Back in 2018, in my second year of studies, long before we ever thought that the 25th Congress would be delayed due to the global pandemic, I applied for volunteering at my first Congress, held in Viminacium. Back then, I had no idea that it would be so important for my future path and interests in the field of Roman archaeology. I am grateful to my colleagues from the Archaeological Institute in Belgrade for allowing me to participate in this major event, even as a volunteer.

When I reminisce about the 24th Congress, I remember all the thought-provoking lectures I absorbed and the interesting people I met, who were young, spirited and always ready to answer numerous questions I had. I will always recall long bus rides during our excursions to southern Serbia, to places such as *Felix Romuliana* or *Naissus*. Even though travel was lengthy, time was well-spent exercising vocal cords (especially in the singing bus) and snacking on famous Plazma cookies in between songs. Our trips had their ups and downs but always ended on a very positive note, oft times with a band playing in the background and a glass of wine in the *Domus Scientiarum* under the stars. One unexpected bonus was an invitation to be a student volunteer on the Pilgrimage of Hadrian's Wall the following summer.

The Twenty-fifth Congress, Nijmegen, the Netherlands 2022

The Congress took place in Nijmegen in the Netherlands in the Roman province of Germania Inferior from Sunday 21 to Saturday 27 August 2022. The pre-Congress excursion started in Münster (Germany) on Thursday 18 August and continued via Krefeld to Nijmegen (Netherlands). The post-Congress tour, from Sunday 28 to Tuesday 30 August, was to Belgium and north-west France.

The Congress was originally planned for August 2021 but delayed by a year due to the COVID-19 pandemic. The organisers felt that the nature of the Congress, with its mix of academic conference sessions, posters, visits to key frontier sites and museums and networking opportunities would not do justice to the subject if it moved to an online platform, like many other conferences during the pandemic. The original 2021 date was marked by an online afternoon 'Road to Limes Congress 2022' preview on Thursday 26 August 2021, with the recording now available online (https://youtu.be/PKLd0bKRYo4).

The principal organiser of the Congress was Harry van Enckevort from the Municipality of Nijmegen, together with Mark Driessen and Carol van Driel-Murray from Leiden University, Erik Graafstal from the Municipality of Utrecht, Tom Hazenberg from the National Roman Maritime Museum and Leiden University, and Tatiana Ivleva from Newcastle University. The Congress beat the previous record of attendees (set at the 23rd Congress in Ingolstadt), with over 440 delegates from 33 countries on four continents. The location for the lectures was the colourful Lindenberg Culture House with a professional event organizer, In-Act Marketing and Organisation, supported by Pauline Jansen from the Municipality of Nijmegen, keeping everything running incredibly smoothly.

The opening session featured welcomes from Harry van Enckevort, the Congress co-chairs (Rebecca Jones and Andreas Thiel) and Jean-Paul Broeren, the Deputy Mayor of Nijmegen, followed by introductions to the Lower Germain Limes World Heritage property (inscribed by UNESCO in 2021) by Jelmer Prins and Erich Claßen. Tatiana Ivleva and David Breeze completed the first session with the launch of the 1st edition of this volume on the History of the Congress and further volumes in the Frontiers of the Roman Empire series (*Dacia, Eastern frontier, Saxon Shore and Maritime Coast, Upper Germanic Limes,* and *Wales*). The authors, translators, illustrators and financial supporters were invited onto the stage to be thanked. The second half of the welcome featured a series of lectures on the Lower German Limes and its highlights from Erik

Graafstal, Steve Bödecker, Harry van Enckevort, Tom Hazenberg, Carol van Driel-Murray, Silke Lange, Stijn Heeren, Boris Alexander Burandt, Wouter Vos, Erik Verhelst and Mark Driessen.

For the first time ever, there were six sessions running concurrently (the previous record was four) – presenting participants with the difficulties of choosing from a wide range of excellent and stimulating sessions.

Most of the Congress sessions were thematic, with some geographically based sessions specific to regions of the empire (including desert areas) and some more general sessions. Given the location of the Congress on the bank of the river Waal, part of the Rhine delta, it is apt that one of the longer sessions was on *Ripae et Litora*, looking at the riverine and coastal edges of the empire. Others were on early frontiers, small finds and dress and adornment, materials, migration, narratives of Roman victory, *vici*, funerary and religion. Contemporary themes of the 21st century were captured in the topics of 'imperialism' and 'childhood' and, of course, the use of cutting edge digital methods for the reconstruction of ancient worlds and the systematic analysis of the growing archaeological datasets. Since the establishment of the FRE, sessions on management and interpretation are now interwoven with other research themes, with sessions on a project between Hadrian's Wall and the Great Wall of China (this was one session that had remote presentations given some difficulties for Chinese scholars to come to Europe), as well as digital data and the complexities of managing a WH property on three continents. For the first time, fitting in with wider discussions on gender in archaeology at a range of international conferences, there was a session on research by and about women.

There were two excursions during the Congress with delegates selecting from a range of tours each day with some aspects the same for all groups. On Tuesday 23 August, crossing the border into Germany, delegates spent considerable time exploring the Archäologischer Park Xanten, Germany's biggest archaeological open-air museum which presents *Colonia Ulpia Traiana,* which also provided food for everyone. The reconstructed amphitheatre provided the opportunity for a photograph of the delegates (Figure 138), taken from a drone. Other sites visited on the different options included the wider Xanten area and Roman camps at Uedem as well as the castellum at Arhnem-Meinerswijk.

On Thursday 25 August, all delegates went to *Castellum Hoge Woerd* (Utrecht) where lunch was served and delegates saw an excellent presentation of a Roman riverboat in the museum (Figure 139). Other visits were to either Fort Vechten (Bunnink) or *NIGRVM PVLLVM* (Zwammerdam) and everyone enjoyed the latter part of the day at the Museum Park Archeon (Alphen aan den Rijn). With reconstructions ranging from early prehistory to the middle ages, most delegates spent time in the Roman section, many cooling their feet on a hot day in the open air Roman pool. This concluded

Figure 138. The Congress participants gathered in the amphitheatre at the Archäologischen Park Xanten, Germany.

Figure 139. The De Meern 1 ship on display at Castellum Hoge Woerd.

Figure 140. The signing of the letter of intent by politicians towards the realisation of a National Roman Maritime Museum at Museumpark Archeon from left to right: Monique Veldman (board member of Foundation Museumpark Archeon), Anouk Noordermeer (alderman of the Municipality of Alphen aan den Rijn), Jack Veldman (director of Museumpark Archeon), Liesbeth Spies (mayor of Alphen aan den Rijn), Arjan de Zeeuw (representative of the Department of Education, Culture and Science), Willy de Zoete (deputy of the Province of South Holland), Jan Jehee (board member of Foundation Museumpark Archeon), Rebecca Jones (co-chair of the International Congress of Roman Frontier Studies), Tom Hazenberg (curator of Foundation Museumpark Archeon) and Andreas Thiel (co-chair of the International Congress of Roman Frontier Studies).

with an event in the arena which included the signing of a letter of intent by local politicians towards the realization of a national Roman Maritime Museum and the presentation of the Zwammerdam ships (Figure 140). It is hoped that this exciting initiative will be visited by a Congress at some point in the future!

Additional initiatives during the Congress included a daily recap in the foyer of the Lindenberg hosted by Tom Hazenberg and providing an overview for delegates on sessions they had missed. On one of the evenings delegates were invited to visit the nearby medieval Saint Nicholas Chapel at the Valkhof for an In Memoriam event where the delegates could present photographs, cards and share their memories of the recently deceased colleagues. Another social event included a tour of the Valkhof Museum where special attention was paid to the fantastic face masks found at Nijmegen. Delegates were also able to visit an exhibition 'Moving Stories. The Riches of the Limes' that linked archaeology and contemporary art connecting the movements of Roman soldiers, traders and craftspeople with stories of modern-day migrants to the Netherlands. This event was accompanied by the presentation of a book on Top

Figure 141. David Breeze receiving his lifetime achievement award.

100 finds from the Lower German Limes (Bruin et al. 2022) and a pop-up exhibition designed especially for the Congress on the spectacular find of a Roman temple at Herwen-Hemeling in 2021.

As has become customary at Limes Congresses, the final closing session saw a series of awards voted for by delegates and also the presentation of a replica of the Face of Nijmegen presented as a lifetime achievement award to David Breeze (Figure 141). At the closing dinner, delegates were treated to a Limes-themed photo booth which produced instant photographs - memorable souvenirs of the Congress.

The pre-Congress excursion took place on 18-20 August with a series of visits in Germany and the Netherlands including to the Museum Varusschlacht in Kalkriese, the Römer Museum in Haltern, the Museum Burg-Linn in Krefeld, the Limburgs Museum in Venlo and the 'Fremdkörper' Neanderthal Museum in Mettmann. The post-Congress excursion on 28-30 August took delegates into Belgium and France with visits including Heerlen, the Gallo-Roman Museum at Tongeren, Bavay (Roman *Bagacum*) and Boulogne Sur Mer, the Roman harbour town of *Gesoriacum*. An alternative single day trip on the 28 August visited the Rijksmuseum van Oudheden (National Museum of Antiquities) in Leiden.

The proceedings of the Congress were very quickly published, just two years after the meeting has taken place, by Sidestone Press in 2024 as four volumes featuring on the cover a spectacular sculpture of a face mask (van Enckevort et al. 2024). This face mask is a 6m high replica designed by artist Andreas Hetfeld of one of the face masks found during the excavations of the Roman Nijmegen and is aptly known as 'The Face of Nijmegen'. It is located on the nearby headland of Veur-Lent and faces the *Ulpia Noviomagus* Roman city of Nijmegen. Steps at the back enable visitors to climb up and look through the eyes of this spectacular sculpture.

Publications

Bruin, J., Eger, Ch., Schmauder, M. and Zandstra, M. (eds), 2022, *Niedergermanischer Limes Top 100 Funde/Neder-Germaanse Limes Top 100 Vondsten/Lower German Limes Top 100 Finds*, Oppenheim am Rhein: Nünnerich-Asmus Verlag.

Jones, R.H. and Thiel, A. 2024 'The 25th Congress of Roman Frontier Studies in Nijmegen' in van Enckevort, H., Driessen, M., Graafstal, E., Hazenberg, T., Ivleva, T. and van Driel-Murray, C. (eds) *Current Approaches to Roman Frontiers (Limes XXV Volume 1). Proceedings of the International Congress of Roman Frontier Studies 1*, Leiden: Sidestone press, 15-22

van Enckevort, H., Driessen, M., Graafstal, E., Hazenberg, T., Ivleva, T. and van Driel-Murray, C. (eds), 2024, *Current Approaches to Roman Frontiers (Limes XXV Volume 1). Proceedings of the International Congress of Roman Frontier Studies 1*, Leiden: Sidestone press

van Enckevort, H., Driessen, M., Graafstal, E., Hazenberg, T., Ivleva, T. and van Driel-Murray, C. (eds), 2024, *Strategy and Structures along the Roman Frontier (Limes XXV Volume 2). Proceedings of the International Congress of Roman Frontier Studies 2*, Leiden: Sidestone press

van Enckevort, H., Driessen, M., Graafstal, E., Hazenberg, T., Ivleva, T. and van Driel-Murray, C. (eds), 2024, *Living and Dying on the Roman Frontier and beyond (Limes XXV Volume 3). Proceedings of the International Congress of Roman Frontier Studies 3*, Leiden: Sidestone press

van Enckevort, H., Driessen, M., Graafstal, E., Hazenberg, T., Ivleva, T. and van Driel-Murray, C. (eds), 2024, *Supplying the Roman Empire (Limes XXV Volume 4). Proceedings of the International Congress of Roman Frontier Studies 4*, Leiden: Sidestone press

Reminiscence

Stéphanie Guédon (France)

Why come, why come back to the Congress? My first experience of a Congress was in Nijmegen in 2022, where and I organized a session together with Rien Polak and René Ployer. I was new in the neighborhood, and I must say all my gratitude to Rien and René for the kindness with which they made me a place. I discovered at the congress forum a space of scientific freedom, and the human exchanges that make it a real community. What better arguments to come back?

Reflections on the Congress

The Congress has no formal constitution. The arrangements for running each Congress lie with the local organising committee, with support provided by an international committee of colleagues who had organised previous Congresses, and two co-chairs, and this has worked well. Each organising committee enjoys considerable flexibility in the organising of its Congress, though a basic framework remains in place. Decisions about the location of each Congress are taken in plenary sessions, led by the co-chairs. During the Ingolstadt Congress in 2015, a questionnaire was issued to all participants seeking their views on the future nature of the Congress: 75% approved the current direction of the Congress (informal set-up; two co-chairs; three-year cycle of meetings, etc).

The structure of the Congress meetings

The structure of the meetings has changed over time. The speakers at the First Congress were all invited and spoke about general issues rather than individual sites. As interest in the Congress grew, attendance gathered pace. The papers were usually a mixture of a few overviews of frontiers together with discussions of forts, army units, inscriptions, coins, small finds and excavations. The typed report of the 1959 Congress in Durham reveals that the papers were divided into thematic sessions: artificial frontiers and their component structures; economic development of the frontier districts; developments of the fourth century; and Rome beyond the frontiers, all presaging later thematic sessions. However, over the following Congresses the subject of many lectures became narrower, often focusing on individual excavations. In order to offer wider prospects, the committee organising the Stirling Congress in 1979 invited specific speakers to provide an overview of work in their province(s) since the last meeting. This initiative has been followed at several Congresses.

In discussion at the end of the Aalen Congress in 1983, a small group decided a new approach was required. As a result, David Breeze organised a thematic session at the next Congress in Carnuntum to consider the impact of the Roman army on indigenous populations. This was so popular that a second session was held on the same evening. In preparation for Canterbury in 1989, Valerie Maxfield and David Breeze considered the shape of the programme and concluded that a useful approach might be some overarching themes based on comparing frontiers in different landscapes. This led to sessions on the problems of desert landscapes in 1989 and river versus artificial frontiers in 1995; as yet no one has risen to the challenge of a general discussion of mountain frontiers. Since Canterbury, nearly all suggestions for themes have come from the delegates themselves rather than the organisers. A popular theme has been 'across frontier' studies allowing the Congress to embrace Roman material and activities beyond the empire; this interest was heralded by Norling-Christensen's paper at the First Congress. The introduction of thematic sessions also allowed topics hitherto rarely considered if at all to enter the curriculum, in particular papers with a gender theme. This started with the session organised by Lawrence Keppie in 1989, 'Realities of frontier life' which included, amongst others, Margaret Roxan on 'Women on the frontiers'. Comparative frontier studies have been explored. The Congress has also extended its reach into looking at cultural resource management issues in relation to Roman frontiers, spurred on by the creation and development of the Frontiers of the Roman Empire World Heritage property. The framework of thematic sessions have gradually overtaken the former framework of the programme so that, at the Congress in Ruse in 2012, the programme was totally structured around themes.

It sometimes appears to be assumed by those who do not attend that the Congress is primarily concerned with the minutiae of army regiments, troops dispositions, the results of small-scale excavations, and the like. While these subjects are important, they are only significant if welded into a greater whole, not least in seeking to determine how frontiers worked. Two wider issues have been discussed almost since the beginning, the purpose of Roman frontier studies and the economies of frontiers. The best example is perhaps Eric Birley's 'Hadrianic frontier policy' delivered at Carnuntum in 1955 in which providing a shield to allow the economic development of the frontier area was the leitmotif of his paper, reflecting the zeitgeist of the post-War years. But this was not the only consideration of the economic aspect of the frontier; a session at the 1959 Congress in Durham was devoted to this theme.

Perhaps most importantly, the focus on themes have brought participants at the Congress to raise their eyes and consider the larger issues, as Colin Wells emphasised in his introduction to the theme of desert frontiers at Canterbury in 1989, thereby forcing delegates to consider wider issues, particularly those beyond Europe. Research into women and the army has been a huge area for exciting research results since the 1990s, as is genderising artefacts. Sessions discussing the urban features of the frontier system, aspects of gender and sexuality of soldiers and civilians ('Small-scale Rome' and 'Sex in the Frontiers' at the Ingolstadt Congress) and the connection between Roman imperialism and the formation of early frontiers ('The creation and reshuffling of tribal (id)entities' at the forthcoming Nijmegen Congress) testify to the health of the discipline. This visible engagement with a broad spectrum of current issues demonstrate how the participants further actively diversify the areas of exploration in frontier studies.

Given this wide array of topics, it is perhaps surprising that some subjects continue to have a rather limited representation. One understudied area has been that relating to archaeological theory, with theoretical perspectives only starting to penetrate Roman army and frontier studies. This can only serve to enrich the discipline in future Congresses.

International influences

Members of the Congress from the beginning have sought to move around the frontiers of the Empire. Tony Birley has pointed out that the location of early Congresses was governed by international politics and these were also reflected in the attendance. The First Congress of 1949 had several poignant elements. Kurt Stade, with whom Eric Birley had planned a Congress for 1940, was unable to attend because he was still a Prisoner of War. Andreas Alföldy had recently fled war-torn Budapest, the post-War influence of the Soviet Union over Hungary having put an end to his research there. His contribution to the Congress, 'The moral barrier on Rhine and Danube', reflected his reaction to the creation of the Iron Curtain. Eric Birley's seminal paper on Hadrianic frontier policy at the Second Congress (mentioned above) could also be seen as a reflection of the existence of the Iron Curtain and the perceived protection provided by the American shield.

A visit to Algeria after 1954 proved to be impossible owing to the start of the Algerian War of Independence. Into the breach stepped Austria, shortly after the signing of the peace treaty in 1955. The following year saw the Hungarian Uprising as well as the Suez Crisis and so Switzerland was a safe option in 1957. Yugoslavia, seeking its own place in the world, was the host in 1961. The stabilisation of Germany led to the Congress first meeting there in 1964, while quietness in the Middle East led to the Israel Congress in 1967 and Amman in 2000.

Other political issues affected the Congress. The transition from colonial rule to independence in North Africa led to an end of the work by Europeans on Roman military installations there and a gradual reduction in the number of papers on that area as the French archaeologists who had led the studies there died. But, on the other hand, the openness of Jordan encouraged more research there, and this led to the Congress in Amman in 2000. In the meantime, some had despaired at a Congress ever being held on the Eastern frontier after Israel in 1967. As a result, a colloquium was organised in Swansea in 1981, followed by Sheffield in 1986 and then a conference in Ankara in 1988. Following that meeting the participants toured the frontier from Gaziantep on the Syrian/Turkish border to Trabzon on the Black Sea and, while a magnificent experience, demonstrated the difficulties of holding a Congress in Turkey at that point. Now, the legionary fortresses at both *Zeugma* and *Samosata* lie below the reservoirs created by the Ataturk Dams.

A major event in the history of the Congress has been the fall of the Berlin Wall. Previously, attendance by colleagues in Eastern Europe had not been easy. One colleague arrived at a Congress in Britain with £2 in his pocket and a suitcase of books which he hoped to sell to pay his way during the meeting. Western institutions were generous in providing grants for colleagues in the former Communist countries to travel to the west, and indeed elsewhere as the British Academy gave a grant to help colleagues from Eastern Europe, Africa and the Middle East to attend the Congress in Amman.

The refugee crisis of 2015, mainly Syrians fleeing their war-torn homeland, peaked in around September of that year, the same time as the Congress was being held in Ingolstadt in Bavaria, southern Germany. A series of border controls enacted by several countries in the Danube region intended to help control the flow of refugees, also affected the ability of some Congress delegates to cross these borders with many arriving late having been held up for days at border crossings. Groups of refugees were camped out at some of the key transport points in Germany, such as Munich railway station. Whilst that was the largest number of refugees into Europe since the Second World War, at the time of completing this book (spring 2022) it is being tragically eclipsed by Ukrainian refugees fleeing the Russian invasion of their country. This also leaves the legacy of scholars from both Ukraine and Russia facing difficulties in attending the 25th Congress at Nijmegen in the Netherlands in the summer of 2022 due to transport and financial limitations.

The cycle of meetings

At the First Congress it had been decided that the meetings should be held on a five-year cycle, which would allow each alternate Congress to be held in Britain, in order to coincide with the decennial Pilgrimage of Hadrian's Wall. This led to UK meetings in Newcastle (1949), Durham (1959), Cardiff (1969), Stirling (1979) and Canterbury (1989). The failure of the proposed Algerian Congress in 1954 broke the pattern, and the eagerness of frontier scholars to meet more frequently led to a Congress being held every two or three years into the 1980s. After the 1989 Congress it was decided to break the link with the Pilgrimage and this allowed the Congress to move to a regular pattern of three years, although again politics intervened to prevent the holding of the agreed Congress in Yugoslavia in 1992. Colleagues in the Netherlands and Belgium stepped into the gap and organised the Congress at Rolduc in 1995. Coincidence allowed the Congress to be held in Newcastle in 2009, 60 years after the first meeting there, with many participants also joining the 13th Pilgrimage of Hadrian's Wall prior to the main Congress. The Nijmegen Congress (August 2022) was originally planned for 2021 but delayed by a year due to the Covid pandemic.

The location of Congresses

There is also a concern to ensure that all parts of the Empire are visited. This led to a Congress in Spain in 2006, and in Bulgaria in 2012, filling in geographical gaps.

Figure 142. Leaflets and books from the 2003 Congress

The Middle East has seen visits to Israel (1967) and Jordan (2000), though a proposed Congress in Morocco in 2018 had to be aborted. The movement of the Congress around the frontiers of the Empire have allowed participants to visit most military sites across its northern frontier. A separate expedition to the frontier in Turkey took place in 1987 as part of the Eastern Frontier Seminar series, an initiative reflecting the paucity of contributions on the Eastern frontier up to that time.

The location of the Congress affects the number of participants. In particular, the central position of Germany in Europe tends to draw more delegates: in Arnoldshain in 1964, Aalen in 1983, and Ingoldstadt in 2015. Amman in 2000 was another peak, probably because of the opportunity it presented to inspect forts normally difficult to access.

The Congresses serve as a useful focus for archaeologists in the host country as well as further afield. Exhibitions are created, books are published and no doubt there will be more digital offers in the future as well. Participants come away with piles of books, leaflets and other paraphernalia from the country visited (Figure 142), and they may

Figure 143. David Breeze receiving his Festschrift in Newcastle in 2009

Figure 144. The celebration for the launch of Bill Hanson's Festschrift in Ingolstadt in 2015

even be arriving with their own material to disseminate which is why quite a few travel by car. The 2003 Congress was notable for the 80th birthday celebrations of Klára Póczy at Aquincum. Festschriften (a collection of writings in celebration of the work of a particular scholar) have been produced in time for publication and presentation at the Congress, often to the surprise of the recipient. Recent examples include research into

Figure 145. Bill Hanson (centre) receiving his Festschrift from two of the editors, Rebecca Jones (left) and David Breeze (right)

Figure 146. Carol van Driel-Murray (centre) receiving her Festschrift from two of the editors, Tatiana Ivleva (left) and Mark Driessen (right) in Viminacium in 2018

the Roman Army and Frontiers presented to David Breeze in Newcastle in 2009 (Figure 143), Understanding Roman Frontiers to Bill Hanson in Ingolstadt in 2015 (Figures 144 and 145) and on Society and Material Culture of the Roman Frontier Regions to Carol van Driel-Murray in Viminacium in 2018 (Figure 146).

Planning a Congress

A Congress attended by up to 350 people requires careful planning. The following two examples demonstrate some of practicalities: for the Stirling Congress in 1979, Brian Dobson and David Breeze held a trial run of the whole programme of site visits in the form of basing their annual Roman frontiers study tour at Stirling University where the Congress was to be held. As a result, potential hitches in the programme were recognised, the timings of the tours tightened and an appreciation gained of how the university operated. A few months before the Congress, the guides undertook a reconnaissance of most of the sites to be visited. For the Amman Congress, there were two prior visits to Jordan to visit the sites, meet the local archaeologists, view the accommodation, talk to the tourist office and, most importantly, meet our patron Prince Hassan. Detailed planning is never wasted and was emphasised when coaches on several other Congresses in the 1970s and 1980s got lost at some point.

As Sebastian Sommer has emphasised, a large number of people are required to help a Congress run smoothly. An organising committee can be small (six in Stirling), but most certainly two people are required for each bus (eight in Ingolstadt) and additional volunteers can be helpful; several have contributed to this book and have progressed to careers in Roman frontier studies. Many contributors require marshalling to produce a handbook. Each lecture room requires supervising. Running a Congress of Roman Frontier Studies is not a task to be undertaken lightly.

In 1974, our colleagues in Lower Germany produced the first handbook, a guide to the frontier to be visited during the Congress. This initiative has been followed by most Congress organisers. These books have enduring value, often providing the most up-to-date information about each frontier area, and becoming 'classics' in their own right.

The growing number of participants has affected the programme. The Mamaïa Congress in 1972 was the first at which parallel sessions were held. In order to relieve the pressure on the programme, poster sessions were introduced at Canterbury in 1989 and these have the added advantage of providing an alternative way in which the results of excavations could be offered for discussion.

Language is an important issue. The main languages have been English, French and German, but Italian, Russian and Spanish have also been accepted. Whereas fifty years ago, the second language of colleagues from Eastern Europe was French or German, now the lingua franca across Europe and especially in younger colleagues is English. In the past, language has been a difficult issue and so brief translations in the other two main languages were provided after each lecture. On one occasion, as the participants anxiously checked their watches in view of the impending lunch, C. E. Stevens neatly summed up a lecture by stating that the speaker had demonstrated that towers at late-Roman forts came in different shapes and sizes at different times, sitting down to resounding applause.

Special features

The logos (Figure 147)

It was not usual for each Congress to have its own logo until the tenth meeting in 1974 which featured one for the first time. This trend was followed by all subsequent Congresses, with logos especially chosen for the occasion, some featuring archaeological finds associated with the Congress location, sponsor, or excursion.

Figure 147. Collage of the logos from the Congresses. From top left: 1974, 1976, 1979, 1983, 1986, 1995, 1997, 2000, 2003, 2006, 2009, 2012, 2015, 2018

The tenth meeting featured an image of a helmet. The depiction is stylised and was designed especially for the Congress by P.J. Tholen, then head of the drawing room of the Rheinisches Landesmuseum Bonn. A helmet of the Hagenau type from Wissel/Niederrhein retained in the museum was used as a model, supplemented by the missing cheek flaps. The use of the helmet as the logo also tied in with the special exhibition of helmets in Xanten. The logo of the 1983 Congress combined the reference to the *Ala II Flavia milliaria* stationed in Aalen with the stylised representation of a *limes* tower. The image of a bull with a ribbon on its horns, logo of the 1995 Congress in Rolduc, derives from the tile stamp from the Tenth Legion found during the excavations (1938-1942) of a part of the Holdeurn tileries in the Nijmegen area. The bull is the symbol of the legion. It was chosen by Harry van Enckevort, then an assistant project leader at the Kops Plateau excavations of the former State Service for Archaeological Investigations (ROB, now RCE), because the Tenth Legion was responsible for the restoration of the Dutch part of the *limes* after the Batavian Revolt. The same logo featured again for the 2022 Congress in Nijmegen, although a different background colour was used: yellow instead of a blue. 2003 in Pécs used the spectacular head of Marcus Aurelius on display in the Janus Pannonius museum. The background image on the logo for the 2009 Newcastle Congress is of an inscription found in 1994 at South Shields Roman fort (*RIB* 3275). It is a centurial building inscription of *legio VI Victrix*, in an ansate panel with legionary standards to either side.

The 'singing' bus

One of the highlights of each Congress, as can be read in many reminiscences, is the invitation to join the 'singing bus'. According to Bill Hanson and the late Sebastian Sommer the tradition was fully established during the Congress in 1986 in Carnuntum as a form of entertainment to survive the long bus rides between stops on the excursions. It has become a regular feature ever since, which will celebrate its 12th iteration at the Congress in Nijmegen in 2022.

According to Carol van Driel-Murray, a regular attender, there was not a single 'singing bus' in the 1980s and '90s. You could choose between an East European bus, where passing round plastic bottles filled with unknown but fiery liquids was common, or an English, German or Dutch language bus. There were strong singers on every bus, drawing upon a shared repertoire of hymns, national and folk songs as well as protest songs of the 1960s and '70s. Carol notes that by 2003 Congress, far fewer people knew all the words, with the late Vivien Swan initiating 'a *limes* song book', which unfortunately (or perhaps fortunately) has never seen the light of day. Because there were fewer people who could still sing and knew all the words, and because many who joined the singing bus were better listeners, subsequent Congresses moved to one principal singing bus, although the main rule of the singing bus appears to be that there are no rules, as well as a willingness to join in the singing.

Figure 148. Tom Parker leads the singing on the bus in 2015

Which of the excursion buses became the singing bus for that day was often established on the spot prior to each excursion and sometimes in secrecy as places might need to be limited if it became popular. An attempt to normalise the singing bus under a designated name board was put forward at Ingolstadt (2015), but was broadly considered to be 'too organised' and therefore not particularly welcomed, which resulted in two singing buses, official and spontaneous, leaving the excursion at Weißenburg. At the Serbian Congress of 2018, it became so popular and due to delegates departing from three different locations, at least three buses were partaking in singing at various points of the Congress.

The 21st century singing bus repertoire includes obligatory songs 'Hotel California', 'California Dreamin', 'Whiskey in the Jar', 'Scarborough Fair', 'What do we do with a drunken sailor', and various songs by the Beatles (Figure 148).

Entertainment: the folk dancing and re-enactors

Throughout the years, Congress participants have enjoyed various forms of entertainment at opening ceremonies, excursions and after a full day of lectures.

Roman military re-enactors are common guests at Congresses, with displays of military dress and equipment, as well as exhibitions of weaponry and material culture. At the Canterbury Congress, the Ermine Street Guard displayed military equipment. During the excursion to Binchester at the Newcastle Congress (2009), the participants were greeted by four re-enactors dressed as a Romano-British woman and three soldiers wearing attire of soldiers in different ranks (Figure 149 and 150). In Ruse, during the visit to the legionary fortress of *Novae* (Svishtov), participants enjoyed a display by the *Legio I Italica*. At the opening ceremony in Viminacium in Serbia, the

Figure 149. Two of the re-enactors greeting Congress participants at Binchester during the 2009 Newcastle Congress

Figure 150. Re-enactors dressed as soldiers greet participants at Binchester during the 2009 Newcastle Congress

Figure 151. Actors following the 'fight' between the Romans and Iron Age people in Viminacium

Figure 152. Children doing traditional dances, sometimes in traditional costume, during the Congress in Bulgaria in 2012 (i and ii); and iii) Congress delegates joining in the dancing in Bulgaria

participants were treated to a spectacle showing a fight between the Roman army and local Iron Age people (Figure 152).

Exhibition of folk dancing has been a feature of Eastern European Congresses: on the excursion days at several Congresses the participants enjoyed watching the dancing of local children dressed in traditional costumes (Figures 92, 152i and ii).

Mementos

These days, Congress delegates come away from the conferences with a wide array of leaflets, information about the Roman province in the country being visited, a specially prepared book for participants and a wonderful array of photographs and memories (Figure 142). Hosts of various Congresses – usually with the support of local sponsors – also designed souvenirs that were given to participants as gifts. These were often local products in the style of archaeological finds from the Roman period, such as pottery. As lasting mementos of the informative and collegiate days spent together, today these decorate the shelves or find their practical use in the office and kitchen. Guests of honour and all those involved in the organisation of the 1983 Congress in Aalen received a heavy cast-iron stove plate from the local ironworks with the depiction of a Roman soldier (dressed in baroque costume); since 1995, brick stamps of the *Legio VII* from Rolduc have been doing their job without complaint as a paperweights; Zsolt Visy had a bowl made stamped with 'MMDCCLVI SOPIANAE' (Figure 153), which since 2003 is still in use today in the household of at least one of the authors. *Sopianae* is the Roman name for Pécs but after some postulating on the date of 2756, it was realised that 2003 was 2,756 years since 753 BC – the traditional date for the foundation of Rome!

Figure 153. The stamped samian bowl from Pécs reading: MMDCCLVI SOPIANAE

A more practical memento from the Congresses has been Congress bags (necessary given the number of books needing to be carried around by the return journey (Figure 154), and one author used to keep a special briefcase just to hold books acquired at a Congress). In a couple of instances (1995 Rolduc; 1997 Zalău), a raincoat or poncho was issued for Congresses in rainier climates. For many delegates, the variety of excursions provides a welcome opportunity to showcase an array of Roman or excavation-themed T-Shirts! (Figure 155).

Inclusivity

Perhaps unsurprisingly, Roman military archaeology and Roman Frontier studies has had a male bias. In 1949, the Scottish archaeologist and numismatist Anne Robertson was the only female speaker out of 11 speakers; in 1957, there were two female

Figure 154. Bags for delegates for the 2018 *Viminacium* and 2015 Ingolstadt Congresses

155i

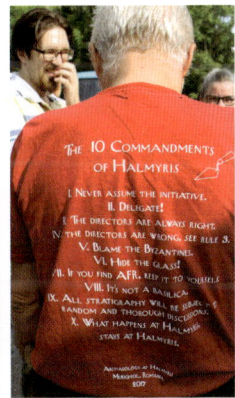

155ii   155iii   155iv

Figure 155. Some of the T-shirts spotted at the Congress: i) Simon Sulk in the 2015 Ingolstadt Limes T-shirt with delegates on the pre-Congress excursion sitting on the steps of Walhalla memorial; ii) Mihail Zahariade models the front and back of the Halmyris excavation T-shirt; iii) Steve Bödecker promoting the Lower German Limes; iv) Rene Ployer publicising the Hadrian's Wall trail

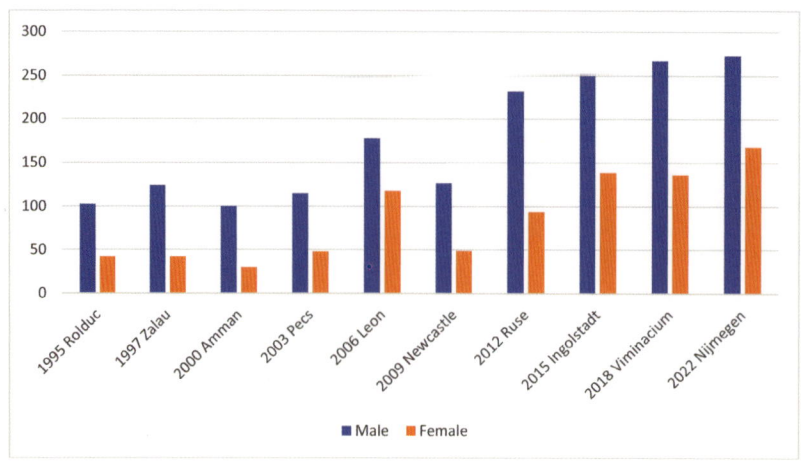

Figure 156. Proportion of male/female delegates in the last 30 years

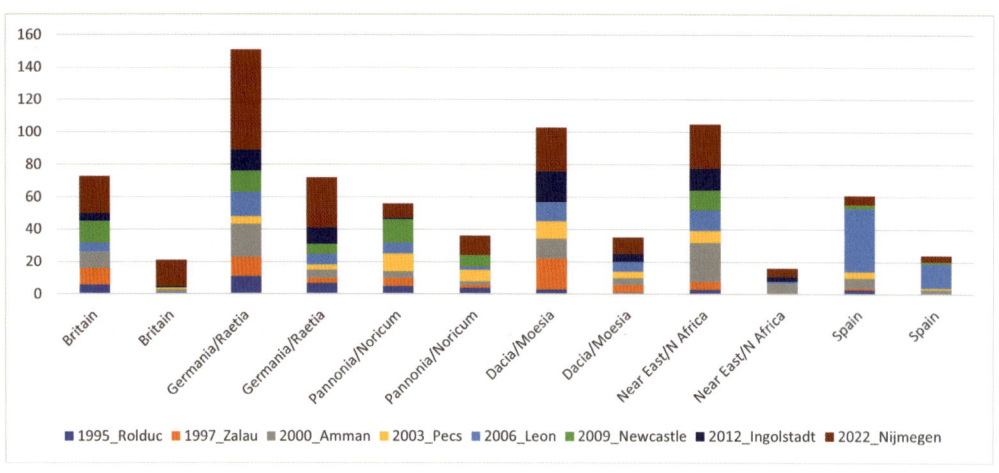

Figure 157. Gender balance by province

speakers out of a slightly larger number of attendees: the numismatist Maria Radnoti-Alföldi and Elisabeth Ettlinger, widely known for her work on Roman Switzerland and Roman pottery. By 1961, 15 percent of attendees were women, but this number was swelled slightly by the presence of several wives of the delegates. It is rather telling that the publication of the Yugoslavian Congress refers to 'The gentlemen whose reports will be accompanied by diapositives [slides] are kindly invited to let us know in advance the size of the respective diapositives', when one of the speakers was a woman. Subsequent Congresses were also dominated by men, with all-male sessions and panels (now known as 'manels') being a common occurrence.

The analysis of the presenters' gender for the past 30 years, since the Congress in Rolduc, shows the proportion of the male:female delegates has consistently been around 7:3 (Figure 156). The Congresses in León, Ingolstadt, Viminacium and Nijmegen have seen some progress in gender balance, with León and Nijmegen seeing a balance of 6:4 and the two recent Congresses seeing a balance of 6:3, but still nowhere near the desired 5:5.

One of the worrying trends that is worth reflecting upon is the involvement of female academics in research on specific geographical frontier zones and topics. This is a matter for consideration that should be appropriately addressed for the state of the discipline as whole. The analysis of the book of abstracts for the past 30 years has shown that while female scholars working on Eastern European, Balkan, Rhine and Danube frontiers are well-represented and visit the Congress on a frequent basis as speakers, chairs and session organisers, when it comes to research on British, Near Eastern and North African frontiers the overwhelming and continuous dominance of male academics is disconcerting (Figure 157). 'Hard' topics considered to be of strictly military nature such as architecture and construction of forts, Roman army and deployment of military units, defence, and the purpose of frontiers have a very strong male academic dominance. There is also an overwhelming majority of male speakers for themes associated with Late Antiquity (Christianity, *limitanei*, late Roman border defence) and contacts beyond the frontier. 'Soft' topics such as supply, consumption, crafts, religion, life and death on the frontiers, presence of civilians, mobility, and material culture are quite well represented for both genders (Figure 158). The latter shows that assumptions on 'traditional' areas frequently studied by women are not entirely correct and 'soft' topics are not 'gender-restrictive', certainly not by comparison to the 'hard' ones. Whilst there is still a dominance of male scholars presenting sites and frontiers and women presenting artefact studies, clearly progress is being made. The Congress in Nijmegen sees a first all-female speakers session *Feminists at the gates. Frontier research by female academics.*

On a positive note, there have always been women involved, and the numbers are slowly but steadily increasing. Helen Adamson, Scottish archaeologist and keeper of Archaeology, Ethnography and History at the Hunterian Museum, Glasgow, was the first woman to join the organising committee of a Congress (1979 in Stirling), joining Gordon Maxwell, Lawrence Keppie, Bill Hanson, and David Breeze. Rebecca Jones was the only female out of four delegates from Scotland to attend the Congress in Amman but by 2015 in Ingolstadt, there were 10 attendees from Scotland, four of whom were female. At the time of writing, Rebecca Jones is co-chair of the Congress, elected together with Andreas Thiel at the Congress in Ingolstadt, the first woman in the history of the Congresses to become the co-chair. Willy Groenman-van Waateringe was chair of the organising committee for 1995 Rolduc; Esperanza Martín Hernández was a major organiser of 2006 León with Ángel Morillo and Suzana Matešić played a key role in organising the 2015 Congress alongside Sebastian Sommer. One of the

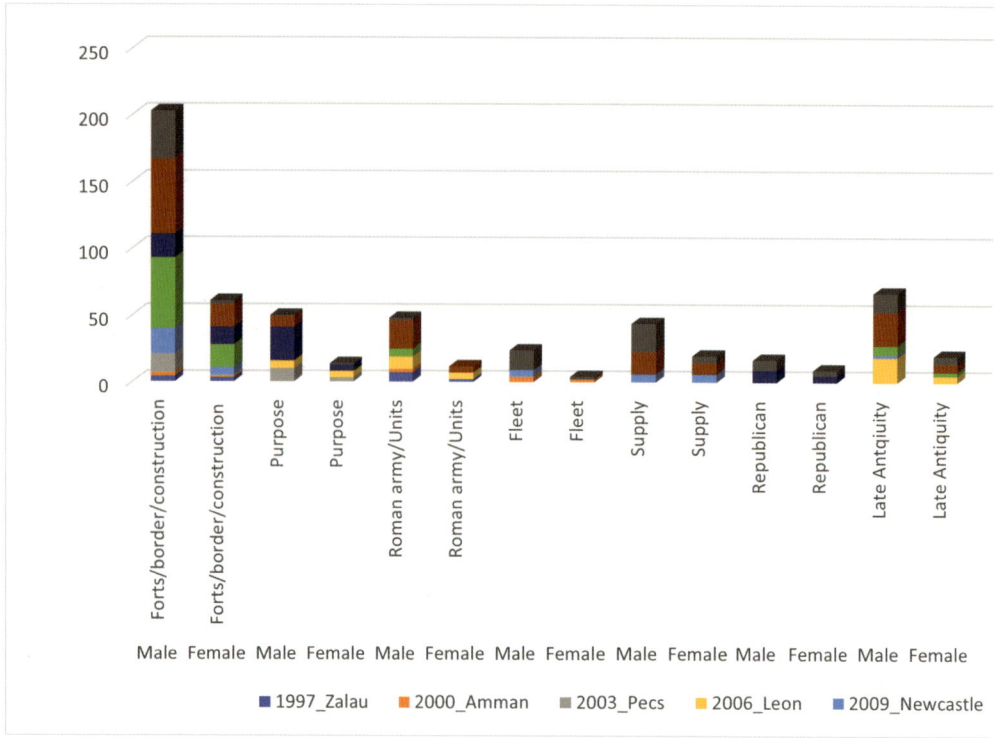

Figure 158. Gender balance by topic

principal organisers of the 2018 Congress in Viminacium was Snežana Golubović from the Archaeological Institute in Belgrade. The Nijmegen scientific committee, responsible for the sessions, excursions and proceedings, had two female members out of six, Carol van Driel-Murray and Tatiana Ivleva. In their reminiscences, many female delegates indicate that gender has never been an issue, and everyone felt welcome and supported by the Limes community. The increasing number of young female scholars attending and presenting at the Congress demonstrates that the subject is in a healthy place.

Many of the accessibility challenges for the Limes Congresses are the same as many other large international archaeological conferences: dominated by Europeans; affordability; timings not always conducive to those with young families; lack of childcare facilities; and long days and long journeys visiting sites in varying locations not easy for those with mobility issues. Cardiff in 1969 was notable for the presence of a child accompanying their parents, Amman in 2000 for the presence of a baby accompanying her mother who was presenting at the Congress (Figure 159). But it is the 2022 Nijmegen Congress that is the first with a written Code of Conduct.

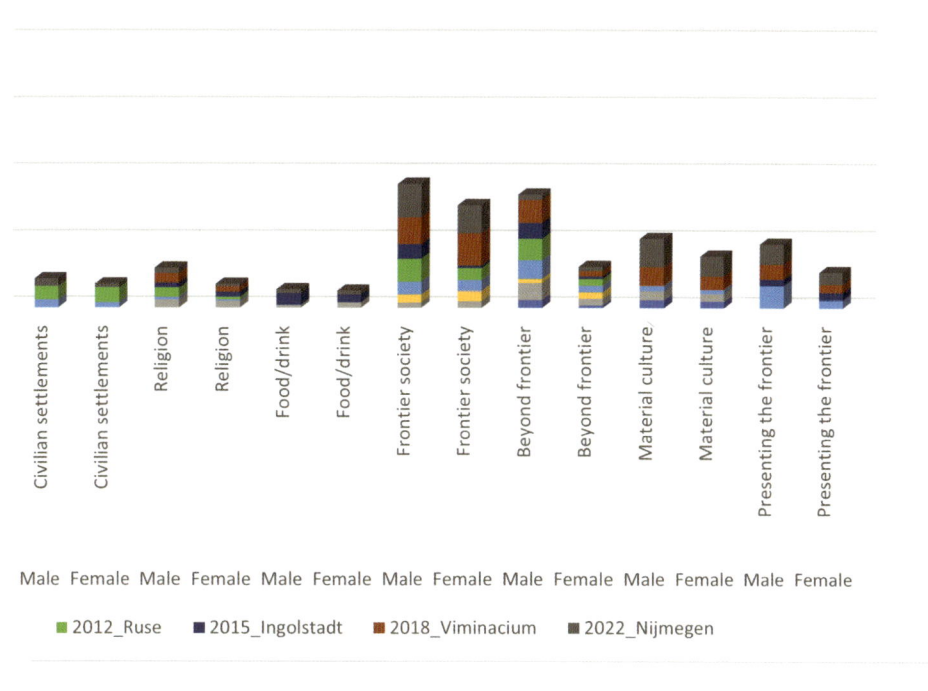

Figure 159. Baby Ariana accompanying her mother Renate Kurzmann to the Limes Congress in Jordan in 2000

A number of recent Congresses have been notable for the number of postgraduate students attending, both Masters and PhD candidates. Ingolstadt was the biggest Congress, with around 400 delegates, partly bolstered by the large number of German students and researchers attending their First Congress and the generosity of the Bavarian State in providing bursaries for young scholars to attend. At the Viminacium Congress, recipients of bursaries not only had their registration fees waived, but also received free accommodation and food at the Congress venue.

A retrospective

David Breeze (UK)

If I was asked to name a single important change over the 17 Congresses I have attended since 1969, it would be the end of the tyrannical rule of elderly professors and the much greater equality between all participants. An element of equality was always present, but it is now prevalent as is evident in the many reminiscences given in this book. In addition, up until 1997, the decision on where to hold the next Congress was taken by a small group behind closed doors; now decisions are held in plenary sessions.

The Congress has also got far better at its attitude to younger colleagues. No longer is it their main duty to carry the bags of their professors! They are encouraged to give lectures (often their first to an international audience as mine was in 1969) and even organise sessions, as several colleagues acknowledge in their reminiscences. Professors such as Willy Groenman-van Waateringe and Alexander Heising have been forceful in encouraging their students to attend the Congress. Many significant lectures have been given at Congresses, as Carol van Driel-Murray notes occurred at Canterbury.

The present open attitude is encouraged by the social milieu of the Congress, especially on the tours. Being ferried across the Danube to visit a fort, driven across the Jordanian Desert in cattle trucks to visit one of the best-preserved Roman forts anywhere, or joining in the festivities on the singing bus where songs in many languages can be heard and even the most distinguished delegates participate, creates a camaraderie which is only strengthened by further participation.

But, at the end of the day, the Congress is about learning more about Roman frontiers – all aspects of Roman frontiers, including the people who lived on them – and in this endeavour face-to-face discussion plays a huge part. The kindness of luminaries form a vital and warm part of my memories of past Congresses, and I have endeavoured to repay their actions through encouraging the friendliness and networking which are such vital elements in our gatherings. The Congress also brought home to me the single necessity of arranging someone to deliver an essential vote of thanks at each venue. When all is said and done, the real heroes are the organisers and their cohorts of helpers as Sebastian Sommer stated, and they all need our special thanks.

The Frontiers of the Roman Empire World Heritage property

The academic discussions and camaraderie of the Congress have played an important part in the development of the Frontiers of the Roman Empire (FRE) World Heritage (WH) property and the wider FRE project. Hadrian's Wall was inscribed on UNESCO's World Heritage list in 1987. Discussions on inscribing other sections of the frontier started at around the millennium leading to the expansion of the inscription to the Frontiers of the Roman Empire with the addition of the Upper German-Raetian *Limes* in 2005 and the Antonine Wall in Scotland in 2008. The idea of one WH property embracing separate monuments in different countries within a framework which encouraged other countries to follow suit was a novel concept. It was embraced by UNESCO and its nomenclature changed to allow the development of the proposal.

In the run up to the German nomination, discussion amongst stalwarts of the Congress of Roman Frontier Studies considered how to move forward and develop the concept of a Frontiers of the Roman Empire WH property. The first step forward was the establishment of a scientific advisory committee formed of the coordinators of the proposed multi-national WH property. Named the Bratislava Group after the location of its first meeting, it sought to set out the framework for the proposed WH property. One early step was the holding of a working party at the Annual Conference of the European Archaeological Association in Thessaloniki in 2002. The impetus was the encouragement by UNESCO for each World Heritage Management System to include a Research Strategy. On the recommendation of Tom Bloemers, six modules were enunciated:

- The creation of an international database relating to the European frontiers of the Roman Empire

- The creation of basic standards of site management for the sites on the frontier

- The definition of gaps in basic information about the frontiers

- The definition of frontier zones (bearing in mind the narrow definition of the 'Hadrian's Wall WH property' and the proposed 'Upper German-Raetian *Limes* WH property')

- The definition of other potential WH properties within the European overarching framework

- Improved public access to information about Roman frontiers.

It was agreed that the achievement of such a programme would require money and the obvious place to seek financial support was the European Union. Sonja Jilck took the lead in applying for funding and obtained a grant from the EU's Culture 2000 programme. The four main objectives of the project were:

- The creation of a web-portal which provides publicly accessible information on all European frontiers
- A series of exhibitions on Roman frontiers
- The improvement of documentation on Roman frontiers
- The formulation of guidelines for the protection, preservation, management, presentation and interpretation of Roman military sites.

The main partners in the project were Roman frontier archaeologists from Austria, Germany, Hungary, Slovakia and the UK, together with Romania, Slovenia and Spain

Figure 160. Frontiers of the Roman Empire Culture 2000 partners at their first meeting in Sopron, Hungary, in 2005. Front row, seated, from left: Esperanza Martín Hernández; Janka Istenič; Piotr Dyczek; Ján Rajtár; Ádam Szentgáli; standing, from left: George Findlater; Rebecca Jones; unknown; Sonja Jilek; Alexandru Matei; Eva Kuttner; C Sebastian Sommer; David Breeze; Andreas Schwarcz; Zsolt Visy; Anton Schabl; Janusz Recław and Klaus Behrbohm

as associate partners (Figure 160). Meetings were held in different locations in the participating countries every four months; other meetings to provide information to colleagues not in the project were also held, for example in the Netherlands (Figure 161). A 200-page report on the Culture 2000 project was published, with a Foreword by Ján Figel, the member of the European Commission in charge of Education, Training, Culture and Youth.

The FRE Culture 2000 project was a stimulus to colleagues who had previously collaborated as archaeologists and exchanged information as academics; now they had to work together as cultural resource managers. In many ways, it is remarkable that the web-portal has survived, now managed by Andreas Schwarcz at Vienna University. This acts as the online home for booklets and maps about Roman frontiers. The Bratislava Group continues its work and the Congress has held sessions on cultural resource management.

Figure 161. Frontiers of the Roman Empire Culture 2000 partners meet with colleagues from the Netherlands at Woerden in 2005, from left: George Findlater, Anton Schabl, Mirjana Sanader, Jürgen Kunow, Jos Bazelmans, Sonja Jansen, Michael Erdrich, Ádám Szentgáli, Paul Wagner, David Breeze, Thomas Becker, Sonja Jilek, Paul Austen, Rebecca Jones, with Tom Hazenberg kneeling

Figure 162. Anna Adamczyk, designer of most of the multi-language books, holding four of the books launched at the Congress in 2022

The new form of collaboration has spawned other projects. One is the multi-language series of books on Roman frontiers. So far, 14 of these have been published with another available online, while a further five are in active preparation (Figure 162). One spin-off from the Culture 2000 project was the production of DVD, 'The Frontiers of the Roman Empire', which includes Jordan as well as the European frontiers, by Erik Dobat and Sandra Walkshofer of *Limesfilm* (edufilm) based in Austria (Figure 163). 70,000 copies were distributed across Europe.

Further EU funding has been utilised for a range of other projects including the Danube Limes Brand, Advanced Limes Applications (Figure 164) and the Living Danube Limes – the latter seeing a replica Roman ship (the '*Danuvia Alacris*') rowing from Ingolstadt in Germany to the Danube delta from July to November 2022 (Figure 165).

Challenges remain. We still have not achieved the creation of a research strategy for Roman frontiers. World Heritage properties do not include archaeological artefacts. Thus, the very material which helps us understand Roman frontiers – inscriptions,

Figure 163. Erik Dobat and Sandra Walkshofer filming in Bulgaria in 2007

sculpture, coins, pottery and small finds – are not protected in this way, though UNESCO is now emphasising the importance of museum collections (Figure 166). And we have yet to embrace the world of Roman frontiers beyond the boundaries of Europe. But a new generation is taking up the reins. Rien Polak has taken over the task of producing accurate maps of frontiers, and, together with Rene Ployer and Ricarda Schmidt, supported by the Bratislava Group, in 2017 produced *The Frontiers of the Roman Empire. A Thematic Study and Proposed World Heritage Nomination Strategy* at the request of ICOMOS, setting a new benchmark for the expansion of the Frontiers of the Roman Empire World Heritage properties. Two more FRE properties were inscribed in 2021: the Lower German *Limes* in the Netherlands and Germany; and the Danube *Limes* (western segment) in Germany, Austria and Slovakia (Figure 167). This is now realising a new concept of a World Heritage 'cluster', and the partners in this initiative will also meet at Limes Congresses in the future to discuss the management of this ground-breaking collaborative initiative.

The discussions do not stop there. The focus for the partners in the FRE WH project has been Europe, but with three sections now inscribed, conversations have started with colleagues in the Middle East and North Africa in order to realise the vision of a FRE WH cluster on three continents. An initiative started by the UK government is seeking closer working relationships between Hadrian's Wall (and also the FRE) and the Great Wall of China (Figure 168) through a project called 'Wall-to-Wall'.

A very real and present threat to the preservation of Roman frontier remains is the impact of climate change. In February 2022, the Climate Vulnerability Index methodology was applied to the Antonine Wall – the first time this newly developed pioneering risk assessment has been applied to either a Roman frontier or an individual component part of a transboundary property. This workshop and resultant report will help inform both the management of the site and set future research priorities.

What have the Romans ever done for us? Those of us involved in Roman frontier studies can attest to a camaraderie and friendship between people from different countries and continents, truly meeting UNESCO's mission for 'intercultural dialogue through education, the sciences, culture, communication and information' and, through that, taking forward our knowledge and understanding of all aspects of Roman frontiers.

Figure 164. Final workshop of the Advanced Limes Applications project in Landshut, Bavaria in 2019 - over 40 participants from around 10 countries across Europe

Figure 165. Building the The 'Danuvia Alacris' replica ship which rowed down the Danube in 2022

Figure 166. The UNESCO World Heritage branding outside the Tullie House Museum and Art Gallery in Carlisle

Figure 167. The UNESCO nomination team for the Danube Limes (western segment) visiting the wall of Regensburg legionary fortress, now incorporated into a multi-storey carpark. From left to right: Markus Gschwind (DE), Katalin Wollák (HU), Zsolt Visy (HU), David Lakin (ICOMOS), Katrin Leicht (Bavarian Ministry), Ruth Pröckl (AT, ministry and UNESCO local point), Rene Ployer (AT), Sebastian Sommer (DE) and Christof Flügel (DE)

Figure 168. Hadrian's Wall visit to the Great Wall of China in 2019 as part of the Wall-to-Wall project. The Hadrian's Wall delegation included: Tony Wilmott; David Breeze; Charles Smith; Barbara Birley; Rob Collins and David Brough. The Chinese delegation included: Zhang Jianwai; Jia Hailin; Zhang Jing; Ma Yanxin; Zhang Bing; Li Tan; Zhang Jun and Huang Siyuan

The Frontiers of the Roman Empire World Heritage property

Further reading

Birley, A.R. 2002. 'Fifty years of Roman frontier studies', in P. Freeman, J. Bennett, Z.T. Fiema and B. Hoffmann (eds), *Limes XVIII, Proceedings of the XVIIIth International Congress of Roman Frontier Studies held in Amman, Jordan (September 2000)*: 1-10. (British Archaeological Reports International Series 1984). Oxford: Archaeopress.

Birley, E. 1974. 'Twenty Years of Limesforschung' in E. Birley, B. Dobson and M.G. Jarrett, (eds), *Roman Frontier Studies 1969. Eighth International Congress of Limesforschung*: 1-4. Cardiff: University of Wales Press.

Birley, E. 1986. 'Limesforschung seit Ernst Fabricius' in C. Unz (ed.), *Studien zu den Militärgrenzen Roms III. 13. Internationaler Limeskongress Aalen 1983*: 17-19. (Forschungen und Berichte zur Vor- und Frühgeschichte in Baden-Württemberg 20). Stuttgart: Kommissionsverlag K. Theiss.

Breeze, D.J. 2017. 'Foreword', in N. Hodgson, P. Bidwell and J. Schachtmann (eds), *Roman Frontier Studies 2009. Proceedings of the XXI International Congress of Roman Frontier Studies (Limes Congress) held at Newcastle upon Tyne in August 2009*: ix-x. (Archaeopress Roman Archaeology 25). Oxford: Archaeopress.

Breeze, D. 2018. 'The value of studying Roman frontiers'. *Theoretical Roman Archaeology Journal* 1: 1-17.

Breeze, D.J. 2020. *The Pilgrimages of Hadrian's Wall 1849-2019: A History*. Kendal: Cumberland and Westmorland Antiquarian and Archaeological Society and the Society of Antiquaries of Newcastle upon Tyne.

Breeze, D.J. 2024. 'Encircling the Empire; How Rome's frontier network was chronicled'. *Current World Archaeology* 125, 40-43.

Breeze, D.J. and Jilek, S. (eds) 2008. *The Frontiers of the Roman Empire, The European Dimension of a World Heritage Site*. Edinburgh: Historic Scotland.

Breeze, D.J. and Jones, R.H. 2020 'The Frontiers of the Roman Empire World Heritage Site', in D. Toncinic, I. Kaic, V. Matijevic and M. Vucov (eds). *Studia Honoria Archaeologica. Proceedings on the occasion of the 65th birthday of Prof. Dr. Mirjana Sanader*, Zagreb: Arheološki zavod Odsjeka za arheologiju Filozofskog fakulteta Sveučilišta u Zagrebu, 63-70.

Breeze, D.J., Jones, R.H. and Oltean, I.A. (eds), 2015. *Understanding Roman Frontiers: A celebration for Professor Bill Hanson*. Edinburgh: John Donald.

Breeze, D.J., Jones, R.H. and Thiel, A. 2021 'The Congress of Roman Frontier Studies: a brief history', in K. Narloch, T. Plociennik and J. Zelazowski (eds), *Nunc decet caput impedire myrto. Studies presented to Professor Piotr Dyczek*, Warsaw: Center for Research on the Antiquity of Southeastern Europe, University of Warsaw, 21-8.

Hanson, W.S. 2009. *The Army and Frontiers of Rome: Papers Offered to David J. Breeze on the Occasion of his Sixty-fifth Birthday and his Retirement from Historic Scotland.* (Journal of

Roman Archaeology Supplementary Series 74). Portsmouth, Rhode Island: Journal of Roman Archaeology.

Hodgson, N. and Griffiths, B., eds, 2022. *Roman Frontier Archaeology – in Britain and beyond: Papers in Honour of Paul Bidwell. Presented on the Occasion of the 30th Annual Conference of the Arbeia Society*. Oxford: Archaeopress.

Ivleva, T., Driessen, M. and Bruin, J. (eds), 2018. *Embracing the Provinces: Society and Material Culture of the Roman Frontier Regions*. Oxford: Oxbow.

Jones, R.H. 2021. 'What divides us also connects us: Roman Frontiers, World Heritage and Community'. *Journal of the Historic Environment: Policy and Practice* 12:2: 120-145. DOI: 10.1080/17567505.2021.1916703

Jones, R.H. 2022. 'The future of cultural resource management on the Frontiers of the Roman Empire World Heritage property', in M. Alberti and K. Mountain (eds) *Hadrian's Wall: Exploring its Past to Protect its Future*. Oxford: Archaeopress, 142-53.

Jones RH, Day JC, McMorrow R, Harkin D, Harkins M, Davies M, Hyslop E and Heron SF 2023 *Climate Vulnerability Index Assessment for the Antonine Wall component of the Frontiers of the Roman Empire World Heritage property*. Historic Environment Scotland, Edinburgh and Climate Vulnerability Index, Townsville www.historicenvironment.scot/aw-cvi

Jones, R.H. and Ivleva, T. forthcoming 2024 'Visible Invisibles: Women and Roman frontiers' in Witcher, R. and Hanscam, E. (eds) *Resistance & Reception: Critical Archaeologies of Iron Age & Roman Worlds*. Oxford: Archaeopress.

Mills, N., ed., 2021. *Visitor Experiences and Audiences for the Roman Frontiers: Developing Good Practice in Presenting World Heritage*. Oxford: British Archaeological Reports.

Ployer, R., Polak, M. and Schmidt, R. 2017. *The Frontiers of the Roman Empire. A Thematic Study and Proposed World Heritage Nomination Strategy*. Vienna / Nijmegen / Munich: Bundesdenkmalamt Österreich/Radboud Universiteit/Bayerisches Landesamt für Denkmalplege

Sulk, S. 2013. 'Von Newcastle nach Ingolstadt – Der XXIII. Internationale Limeskongress findet 2015 in Bayern statt'. *Berichte der Bayerischen Bodendenkmalpflege* 54: 183–90.

Sulk, S. 2015. 'Ingolstadt im Zentrum der Limesforschung - Der Limeskongress 2015 stellt neue Rekorde auf'. *Denkmalpflege Informationen* 162: 87–90.

Zsidi, P (ed.) 2003. *Forschunger in Aquincum 1969-2002: zu Ehren von Klára Póczy*. Budapest: BHM Aquincum Museum, Aquincum Nostrum II. 2.

Appendix

The frontiers of the Roman Empire multi-language books

Published by Archaeopress: www.archaeopress.com

Editor David J. Breeze

Breeze, D.J., Jilek, S. and Thiel, A. 2005. *Frontiers of the Roman Empire/Grenzen des Römischen Reiches/Frontières de l'Empire Romain*. Edinburgh, Esslingen and Wien.
Dyczek, P. 2008. *The Lower Danube Limes in Bulgaria*. Warsaw and Vienna. Second edition 2024.
Harmadyová, K., Rajtár, J. and Schmidtová, J. 2008. *Slovakia/Slowakei/Slovensko*. Nitra.
Visy, Zs. 2008. *The Roman Limes in Hungary/A Római limes in Magyarországon*. Pécs. Second edition 2011.
Breeze, D. J. 2009. *The Antonine Wall/Der Antoninus Wall*, Edinburgh. Second edition 2022.
Jilek, S. 2009. *The Danube Limes, A Roman River Frontier/Der Donaulimes Eine Römische Flussgrenze*. Warsaw. Out of print.
Breeze, D.J. 2011. *Hadrian's Wall/Der Hadrianswall/Le Mur d'Hadrian*. Hexham. Second edition 2023.
Jilek, S., Tuttner, E. and Schwarcz, A. 2011. *The Danube Limes in Austria/Der Donaulimes in Österreich*. Wien. Second edition 2023.
Mattingly, D., Rushworth, A., Sterry, M. and Leitch, V. 2013. *The African Frontiers/Die Grenzen in Afrika/Les frontières africaines*. Edinburgh. Also in Arabic.
Korać, M., Golubić, S., Mrđić, N., Jeremić, G. and Pop-Lazić, S. 2014. *Roman Limes in Serbia/Rimski Limes u Srbiji*. Beograd.
Graafstal, E.P., Williams, W.H.W. and Bödecker, S. 2018. *The Lower German Limes/De Nedergermaanse Limes/Der Niedergermanische Limes*, Leiden.
Reddé, M. 2021. *The Roman Frontier in Egypt/La frontière romaine en Égypte*.
Marcu, F. and Cupcea, G. 2021. *The Roman Frontier of Dacias/Frontierere Romane ale Daciei*.
Becker, T., Roth, S. and Thiel, A. 2022. *Upper Germanic Limes/Der Obergermanische Limes/ Le Limes der Germanie Supérieure*.
Abudanah, F., Braund, D., Driessen, M., Konrad, M. and Polak, M. 2022. *The Eastern Frontiers/Les frontières orientales*. Also in Arabic.
Wilmott, T., Vanhoutte, S. and Bridgeland, R. 2022. *The Saxon Shore and the Maritime Coast/Le litus Saxonicum et la côte maritime*.
Guest, P. 2022. *The Roman Frontiers in Wales/Ffiniau Rhufeinig Cymru*.
Breeze, D.J. 2023. *The Hinterland of Hadrian's Wall/ L'arrière-pays du mur d'Hadrien*.

Karasiewicz-Szcypiorski, R. and Mamuladze, S. 2024. *The Roman Frontier in Georgia.* Batumi and Oxford.

Fischer, T., Fischer, V., Flügel, C., Gschwind, M. and Meyer, M. forthcoming. *The Roman Frontier in Raetia/Die römische Grenzen in Räetian.*

Not in the series:

Tentea, O. and Matei-Popescu, F. 2016. *Between Dacia and Moesia. The Roman forts of Muntenia under Trajan.* Cluj Napoca: Mega.

Vizy, Z. 2011. *Romans on the Danube. The Ripa Pannonica in Hungary as a World Heritage Site.* Pecs: University of Pecs.

Acknowledgements

The authors are also extremely grateful to the following for the use of images: Museum Augusta Raurica (12 & 13); the Birley family (3 & 11); Alexander Boris Burandt (129); Deutsche Limeskommission / Simon Sulk (119, 120, 155i); Hans Doderer (140); Mark Driessen (146); Durham University Journal for 1930 (2); Sven van Efferen (141, 165); Thomas Grane (126, 127); Sebastian Held (138 and cover image); Ortolf Harl (110, 112, 152i); Alexander Heising (121); Brenda Heywood (7); Nick Hodgson (107); The Herald (Glasgow) (9); Sonja Jilek (81); Dmitry Karelin (152iii); Renate Kurzmann (159); Orsolya Lang (133); Library collection, University of Groningen (19); Felix Marcu (96, 113, 114); Nemanja Mrđić (134); Tom Parker‡ (51, 52); Rene Ployer (167); Simon Sulk (4); Tullie House Museum & Art Gallery (8, 11 and cover image); Leo Verhart (10); Nina Willburger (89); John Peter Wild (14); Tony Wilmott (168); Susanne and Heinrich Zabehlicky (43, 44, 45, 46, 47, 54, 55, 56, 57, 58, 61, 65, 76, 105, 107, 109, 128, 135); Suzanne Zahel (94, 103, 124, 128, 136). All other images are those of the authors or unknown provenance.

Figure 169. The organisers of the Nijmegen and Batumi Congresses after the closing ceremony in Nijmegen in August 2022. Second row, from left to right: Carol van Driel-Murray, Piotr Jaworski, Radek Karasiewicz-Szczypiorski, Natalia Lockley, Karolina Trusz, Tatiana Ivleva, Emzar Kakhidze, Martin Lemke, Harry van Enckevort, Mark Driessen. First row: Zaur Akhvlediani, Tom Hazenberg, Erik Graafstal, Lasha Aslanishvili, Maciej Czapski.